D0629093

"Frances Kai-Hwa Wang languages desire with a refreshing candor and mischievous wit. She talks story of divorce, of messy relationships, and of enduring humiliating racist and misogynistic microaggressions because she is an Asian American woman. Wang's prose poems and lyric essays ring with wisdom and hard-earned truths and dreamlike reveries in this unforgettable collection."

—May-lee Chai, author of *Useful Phrases for Immigrants: Stories*, winner of the American Book Award

"'I do not know if one ever recovers from Kathmandu,' the speaker in one of Frances Kai-Hwa Wang's poems ruminates, and I don't know if we ever recover—or want to recover—from *You Cannot Resist Me When My Hair Is in Braids*, which is part of the marvelous linguistic spell that is cast in this book. By turns whimsical, romantic, witty, hybrid, self-deprecating, fierce, intertextual, hashtagged, polylingual, and full of a radiant empathy that connects us to Vincent Chin, George Zimmerman, Sun Ku Wong, Hanuman, and Milan Kundera, this is a collection that astounds, surprises, and delights, which encapsulates much of what a book that leaves an indelible mark should do. Yay Frances for a collection that rocks!"

—Dr. Ravi Shankar, Pushcart Prize–winning author of *Correctional*

"*You Cannot Resist Me When My Hair Is in Braids* is a great gathering of the many contradictions, the multifaceted multitudes, of Frances Kai-Hwa Wang. Across its pages of aphorism, prose poem, micro-fiction, and lyric essay, we encounter Patsy Cline heartache and AOC outrage, delivered in a humor that is solely Wang's own."

—Tim Tomlinson, director and cofounder of New York Writers Workshop, author of *Requiem for the Tree Fort I Set on Fire* and *This Is Not Happening to You*

You Cannot Resist Me
When My Hair
Is in Braids

Made in Michigan Writers Series

General Editors

Michael Delp, Interlochen Center for the Arts
M. L. Liebler, Wayne State University

A complete listing of the books in this series can
be found online at wsupress.wayne.edu.

You Cannot Resist Me
When My Hair
Is in Braids

Frances Kai-Hwa Wang

WAYNE STATE UNIVERSITY PRESS
DETROIT

ISBN 978-0-8143-4941-0 (paperback)
ISBN 978-0-8143-4942-7 (e-book)

Library of Congress Control Number: 2021951007

Publication of this book was made possible by a generous gift from The Meijer Foundation.

Cover art and design by Kristle Marshall

Photographs in "Dreams of the Diaspora" and "Texting Nostalgic for Kathmandu" by Jyoti Omi Chowdhury. Photographs in "Sowing Aunties" by Frances Kai-Hwa Wang.

This is a work of creative nonfiction that stands at the intersection of lyric essay and prose poetry. It is a hybrid work of literature with elements of both fiction and nonfiction. It reflects the author's recollections and reflections on experiences over time. Some names, places, events, incidents, details, and identifying characteristics have been changed; some characters have been combined; some dialogue has been re-created; and time and space have been condensed and rearranged. Other names, places, characters, dialogue, characteristics, details, events, and incidents are a product of the author's imagination. Any resemblance to actual persons, living or dead, or actual events is purely coincidental.

Wayne State University Press rests on Waawiyaataanong, also referred to as Detroit, the ancestral and contemporary homeland of the Three Fires Confederacy. These sovereign lands were granted by the Ojibwe, Odawa, Potawatomi, and Wyandot nations, in 1807, through the Treaty of Detroit. Wayne State University Press affirms Indigenous sovereignty and honors all tribes with a connection to Detroit. With our Native neighbors, the press works to advance educational equity and promote a better future for the earth and all people.

Wayne State University Press
Leonard N. Simons Building
4809 Woodward Avenue
Detroit, Michigan 48201-1309

Visit us online at wsupress.wayne.edu.

With gratitude to my parents and elders,
who are still trying to set me up

For my children, who are not allowed
to date until they are 35

Contents

Notes and Acknowledgments

"Did you eat? means . . . I Love You." was previously exhibited, with the photography of Hao Hao Wang, at the Blacklava 20th Anniversary Art Exhibition at Hatakeyama Gallery, Los Angeles, in August 2012; was originally published, with the photography of Hao Hao Wang, in *Kartika Review*, issue 14 (Fall 2012): 63–66; was previously exhibited, with the photography of Hao Hao Wang, at the Asian American Women Artists Association (AAWAA) in May 2013, SOMArts, San Francisco; and was reprinted in the *Dreams of the Diaspora* chapbook by Frances Kai-Hwa Wang, January 2014.

"Dreams of the Diaspora" was written for and previously exhibited in a multimedia art installation created with Jyoti Omi Chowdhury at the Smithsonian Asian Pacific American Center Indian American Heritage Project in an online gallery (https://www.si.edu/object/yt _KNv_fUYv7Dc) and in a traveling art exhibition on the H-1B visa at Twelve Gates Art Gallery in Philadelphia, January 2014; and reprinted in the *Dreams of the Diaspora* chapbook by Frances Kai-Hwa Wang, January 2014.

"Texting Nostalgic for Kathmandu" was originally published, with photographs by Jyoti Omi Chowdhury, in *Cha Asian Literary Journal*, Hong Kong, issue 23 (March 2014); and reprinted in in the *Dreams of the Diaspora* chapbook by Frances Kai-Hwa Wang, 2014.

"Tsundere Pride or You Are So Prickly!" was written for and performed at the *Navigating the underCurrents* activist poetry reading curated by May-lee Chai, inspired by an art installation by Stella Zhang in the AAWAA's *underCurrents & the Quest for Space* multidisciplinary arts exhibition, at SOMArts in San Francisco, May 2013; and originally published in the *Dreams of the Diaspora* chapbook by Frances Kai-Hwa Wang, 2014.

"Poignant Truth, Precarious You (and Preparing for the Sriracha Apocalypse)" was written for and performed at EATING CULTURES: Literary Sriracha—A Spicy Mix of Poetry, Mini-Memoirs, and Flash Fiction, curated by May-lee Chai, inspired by an art installation by Jung Ran called *Poignant Truth*, in the AAWAA's Eating Cultures Exhibition, at SOMArts in San Francisco, May 2014; and originally published in *Drunken Boat*, issue 23 (April 2016).

"A Suggestion of Salt" was written with Ravi Shankar and first performed at the Matwaala South Asian Poetry Festival, April 27, 2017, at Asian American Writers' Workshop, New York City; and originally published in *Knights Library Magazine* (Spring 2020).

"The Californian" was originally published in *Third Wednesday Journal* 12, no. 1 (2019), and designated a poem of considerable merit.

"Secret Crush" was originally published in *Cha Asian Literary Journal*, Hong Kong, issue 35 (March 2017).

"Down in the Basement of the DIA" was first performed at 2018 Cracked Walnut Lit Fest Stargazers reading in St. Paul, June 2018, and was originally published in the Cracked Walnut anthology, *After the Equinox*, 2019.

"Whatever Happened to 王大中 (Wang Da Zhong)?" was written for and first performed at *IS/LAND That We Walk* dance performance in Ann Arbor, February 2019, and originally published in *Chrysanthemum—Voices of the Taiwanese Diaspora II*, by TaiwaneseAmerican.org, 2021.

"Talkin' to Whypipo" was first performed at Ann Arbor Poetry's Slammiversary, October 2019, and was originally published in *Meridian: The APWT Drunken Boat Anthology of the Best New Writing from the Asia Pacific and Beyond*, edited by Sally Breen, Ravi Shankar, and Tim Tomlinson, by Asian Pacific Writers and Translators (APWT) and *Drunken Boat*, December 2020.

"Crying on Airplanes" was first performed at 2018 Cracked Walnut Lit Fest Stargazers reading in St. Paul, June 2018, and was originally published by *Knights Library Magazine* (Fall 2019) and nominated for a Pushcart Prize.

"Finding Home Between the Vincent Chin Case and COVID-19" was written for and performed at Detroit Public Television "Asian Americans: The Detroit Story" and originally published in *High Stakes Humanities* by University of Michigan Press Fulcrum, 2021.

An early version of "Learning to Drive Defensively" was exhibited in the University of Michigan Diversity Equity and Inclusion Summit Creative Gallery, October 2020.

An early version of "Breath Rises" was included in an Ann Arbor District Library and University of Michigan Library pandemic mail art project, summer 2020; will be exhibited after the pandemic; and will be included in an artist book as part of the *Artists' Books Collection* in the Book Arts Studio at the U-M Library.

"You Cannot Resist Me When My Hair Is in Braids" was originally published in the *Imaginary Affairs—Postcards from an Imagined Life* chapbook by Frances Kai-Hwa Wang, 2012.

An early version of "Sowing Aunties" was first exhibited and performed at the AAWAA and Asian Pacific Islander Cultural Center Sowing Agency Seeding the Future for Environmental Justice Art Exhibition, San Francisco, April–May 2021; won the 2021 APWT and *Joao-Roque Literary Journal* Asia Pacific of the Mind Award; and was originally published in *Joao-Roque Literary Journal*, issue 20 (Summer 2021).

An early version of "Lost Constellation" was previously published in University of Michigan Museum of Art *Art in your Inbox*, March 2021; performed with IS/LAND Asian American performance collaborative for Detroit Institute of Art, *Lost Constellation (Pt. 1 + II) / IS/LAND*, May 1, 2021; and broadcast on Detroit Public Television (DPTV) *One Detroit* during an interview with Will Glover, May 17, 2021.

Many thanks to Annie Martin, Joe Grimm, Amna Nawaz, Traci G. Lee, Tracie D. Hall, Joz Wang, May-lee Chai, Kate Agathon, Grace Hwang Lynch, Tamiko Wong, Dawn Lee, Tanzila Ahmed, Katherine Reynolds Lewis, Chandra Thomas Whitfield, Janet Cho, Thien-Kim Lam, Jen Shyu, Chien-An Yuan, Ayesha Ghazi, Rohin Guha, Jie-Song Zhang, Jyoti Omi Chowdhury, Ravi Shankar, Bryan Thao Worra, Patrick Landeza, Tom Peek, Catherine Robbins, Charley Sullivan, Susan Najita, Amy Stillman, Kaori Ohara, Sujata Shetty, Lisa Kohn, Rich Evans, Daphne Lin, Ryan Suda, Phil Yu, Jeff Yang, Simon Mermelstein, Jason B. Crawford, Leslie McGraw, Smithsonian Asian Pacific American Center, AAWAA, Asian American Writers Workshop, APWT, New York Writers Workshop, Matwaala South Asian Poetry Festival, Ann Arbor Poetry, Cracked Walnut Lit Fest, TaiwaneseAmerican.org, *Kartika Review, Cha Asian Literary Journal, Drunken Boat, Knights Library Magazine, Third Wednesday Journal,* Ann Arbor District Library, IS/LAND, University of Michigan, Washtenaw Community College, University of Hawai'i Hilo, Volcano Art Center, Ann Arbor Chinese Center of Michigan, American Citizens for Justice, Knight Foundation, Ann Arbor Area Community Foundation, CultureSource, DPTV, Bookbound Bookstore, TK WU, Eastern Accents, Sweetwaters Café, my parents, my aunties, and many more.

Prologue

Buddhists say that suffering comes from unsatisfied desire, so for years I tried to close the door to desire. Any desire. I was so successful, I not only closed the door, I locked it, barred it, nailed it shut, then stacked a bunch of furniture in front of it.

It was the only way I could survive the long loneliness that was my marriage. I was dead to desire, going through only the motions of life. I did not even dare read novels, write poetry, or watch bad romantic comedies for fear of what small hope they might inspire.

And now that door is open, wide open, and all my insides are spilling out.

And you, not knowing this dangerous detail, tease me, dare me to live again.

The more I warn you away, the closer you draw toward me. I fear you will catch fire, that I will consume you, that I won't be able to stop.

A friend remarks about my former car and former life, "I saw a Land Rover broken down on the side of Highway 23 and thought of you."

So glad that ain't me anymore!

"Strut and unfurl," you tell me.

And courage comes.

Frances Kai-Hwa Wang
Ann Arbor, 2022

DREAMS OF THE DIASPORA

Amused by my earnestness, you ask, "Does the diaspora dream?" Of course the diaspora dreams! Many dreams. Full of hunger and longing, lingering and remembering. Trying to recapture what never was. As time keeps moving us farther and farther away from home.

"But those are not really dreams are they. Those are longing . . . remembering . . . hunger . . . and dissolution. Dreams are inherently about the future, not about the past. So the diaspora does not dream but yearns to dream."

I was born in the slipstream of the diaspora. The diaspora is my home. I have no memories of playing back-alley cricket. My father is the one who walked barefoot to school with his shoes around his neck, not I. I know the stories of Brer Rabbit as well as I do the *Mahabharata*. I love a good cup of chai early in the morning mist, but I can never get the spices quite right, so I am relegated to the prepackaged chai at my neighborhood Sweetwaters Café.

But I know wherever I am in the world, I can approach certain strangers, my hands to my forehead, "Auntie," "Uncle," "Grandmother," and find safe haven and a good meal. The cute desi boy at the market slips me a tiny sample of pickle that his mother made and mailed to him.

You do not understand. You have an answer when people ask, "Where are you from? No, where are you really from?"

I was born here. But I feel so far from home.

My family keeps marching forward, very clear on what they want. A safe home. A stable job. Good schools. Enough money to provide for both the older and younger generations. They have had enough of war and poverty. They pay their taxes and laugh at my youth when I talk of justice and fair representation.

Yet they know all the rules and regulations and shortcuts and loopholes for visas, green cards, naturalization. Even Grandmother is studying her phonetic cheat sheet to pass the U.S. citizenship exam in a language she does not speak. They tell me I can even be president someday, because I am a natural-born citizen.

I am the dream of the diaspora, but I am lost.

You take my hand in yours and say, "You do not appreciate how much that blue passport you were born into protects you, how much the fairness of your skin insulates you. I walked across so many countries and studied hard for so many years to reach this place. Finally. New York City. University. Graduate school. Work. More work. The lady in the harbor called out to me.

"Then those planes fell out of the sky, and she looked away.

"I also see aunties and uncles and grandmothers . . . at the airport, being pulled off planes . . . yards of sari and turban fabric unwound onto the floor. I watch as friends laugh along nervously with their bosses' and coworkers' terrorist jokes, dare not speak out for fear of losing their H-1B. I go to birthday parties and picnics in the park that are interrupted by the FBI responding to reports of suspicious activity. They check our chicken biryani for explosives.

"I register my name and address so they can find me if they need to arrest me."

Restless, curious, wandering, I walk the crowded cities and open land-
scapes of the world, searching for meaning and a place to call home, and
instead, I find you.

Walking with you, I find myself.

Walking with you, I feel a little less lost.

Walking with you, I begin to dream my own dreams.

PUBLIC PERSONA

I like being in public with him, the physicality of it, all wool coats and leather boots.

Solid.

Present.

No one looks through me when I am with him.

Tsundere Pride or You Are So Prickly!

OH! YOU. ARE. SO. PRICKLY!

I am ready to throttle you constantly.

"Throttle me?" You are intrigued. "Explain."

I don't understand how infuriated I get almost every time I talk with you. I don't bicker with anyone else the way I bicker with you. When I summon up my best courage to tell you what I want, straight, you answer my question with a question, turning my certainty into angst.

Again.

"Really!" You ask, "How do I infuriate you? Does infuriating you make you hot?"

OH! CAN'T. TAKE. YOU. ANYWHERE!

There is an edge to your humor that I cannot figure out: if you are actually a jerk underneath or if you are actually nice underneath, pretending to be a jerk.

"Hmmm, could be both," is your answer. "Circumstances dictate the level of clarity in action. The rest is just hubris."

WTF does that even mean?

What happened to you that you are so careful with your heart? I catch glimpses of it, glimmers, when you turn off the stereo while your father prays, in the wry smiles of the children captured in your photographs. But just when I begin to think I see, in your stories, in your touch, in that marvelous space that opens up between us, you divert me into a joke or into a random long string of words, and you wrap your heart back up again inside your prickly, spiky, pointed armor.

Tsundere.

When I met the third great love of my life, I was totally open to his words of hope and possibility. I was innocent, naïve, trusting. At the time, I did not know how to be otherwise.

I waited for the usual warning signs, the "Hey, China Doll," and "Konnichiwa, Baby."

When they didn't come, I finally let myself fall in love on a Sunday afternoon in the sunshine while walking past the dinosaur museum.

And then he was gone.

So I began to protect myself, to act tougher than I was, to retreat into myself. Overnight, I sprouted spikes across my shoulders and down my sides, and I hid them by turning them inward, onto myself, and I hated the person I became. Loud. Phony. Posturing. Tough. Tsundere.

The next few fellows had no chance.

By the time I met you, the banter was rehearsed, the defenses were strong, I had no interest.

But you were persistent.

Teenage girls gather around my kitchen table, making mochi and crying over boys. I hear the same useless advice that my girlfriends give to me, "Boys are dumb. Let him go." One teenager draws me a diagram in the scattered mochiko to explain the seriousness of the situation: A loves B who loves C who is going out with D who cheated on E in seventh grade (whatever that means) who made a pass at F who got herpes from G who is not allowed to date but likes H who might be gay and has a crush on J who held hands with K who is chatting with L on Facebook who follows M on Tumblr who keeps texting A at midnight . . .

When one girl exclaims, "I wish they would just all go to Antarctica!" Another one answers, "That's chill."

At night I dream the rhythm of your breath.

At the Midwest Asian American Students Union Conference, two speakers in two separate conversations remark to me how comfortable they feel here in the embrace of over one thousand Asian American college students, how different this feels than their everyday life where they swim upstream daily, how much they ache for this to be "normal."

I am struck because I live and work in Asian America. I have constructed an Asian American community around me, and I choose when to step out into the mainstream.

I was so naïve when I first came to the Midwest. I was so slow to learn what it was like to be a minority. I did not understand how the lens of stereotype functions. Once, when facing down a big Main Street lawyer who could not see me, could not hear me, could not comprehend the very complicated difference between Chinese New Year and Lunar New Year, I realized his confusion came from me not fitting expectations. I tried to explain, standing up tall in my suit, piling on words and more words, big words, eloquent words, but without an accent, he just could not understand me. I finally had to let go of who I am in my world, in Angry Asian America, and become small, delicate, porcelain, quiet, the exotic Oriental china doll he could understand. I retracted my spikes into myself (ouch), pretended to be someone I was not, and, for a moment, saved myself.

Then I think about the questions being asked about the two brothers in Boston after the marathon. At first, everyone was asking, "What happened to these two boys in their experience of the American dream?" (*Boys?* Nineteen and twenty-six years old and still *boys*? Ah, that was back when they were still white. Troubled Seung-Hui Cho, twenty-three, and immature Dharun Ravi, eighteen, were never described as *boys*.) The brothers are initially described by friends as *sweethearts, nice, good athletes*. People joke about *brofiling* until they discover that (gasp) there are Muslims in Chechnya. Never mind that Chechnya is exactly in the middle of the Caucasus. Suddenly they become Brown.

Imagine that happening every day of their lives.

A grandfather gives his granddaughter dating advice: "Those bombers looked nice, so be careful with nice-looking boys, because they could turn out to be terrorists."

This country is hard on outsiders.

I wonder if it was hard on you.

The last time you were here, I sensed a moment of vulnerability behind your hubris, and I was amazed to watch as a space of lightness and possibility opened up between us.

I feel an ease with you I do not feel with anyone else.

You do not know how much we are alike. Not just the smoothness of our skin, the color of our hair, the cadence of our languages. The smell of jasmine permeates my memories of you.

You notice the Milan Kundera on my nightstand and remark that that is your favorite book. Hey, mine too. What are the chances? I want to burrow into this moment and talk to you about the ideas in the book—I am dying to understand how your mind works—but instead, I blurt out an old story about a French geographer who once loved me until we got into a fight over Kundera. And the moment is over. And the already widening gap between us widens even more.

I then trot out all my usual stories, old stories, public stories, stories where I posture and pose myself into bravado. When really, all I want to do is write new stories with you, quiet stories, private stories, stories I do not publish or perform in front of strangers.

I could be a safe space for you.

I tell the others that I am not terribly serious, certainly not reliable. Reckless. Irresponsible. I cannot even guarantee who I will be a few days from now. "Tread carefully," I tell them, "I am not nice."

But with you, I find a quiet moment of courage, clear eyes and steady hand, discovering who it is I am supposed to be, creating myself anew.

I am resigned to the heartbreak I know will come in the end with you, but somehow, I am able to let go of my spiky prickly crustiness, my tsundere pride, and simply stand here naked before you.

I like who I am when you are in my heart.

Texting Nostalgic for Kathmandu

Y ou text me from the airport.

I text back just as I clear security.

I always write to you from airports. I know that I will find you here.

With the shorthand of airport codes (DAC, CCU, DEL, KTM, DTW, ORD, LAX, ITO), we catch each other at transfer points, reach out to each other until the doors finally close and tray tables must be stowed and all electronic devices must be turned off.

Today you are heading to the ancient city of my youth while I am disappearing into summer, fire, and sea.

I marvel over Google Maps, how much the city has grown. I used to live in Baluwatar, up the hill behind the Russian Embassy, in a little yellow house with a garden overlooking the city.

Kathmandu.

Every day, I used to plunge down that hill on my bicycle, head down, knees tucked, braids and purple chiffon scarf flying. The only girl on a bike in town, everyone knew who I was. I biked furiously across the city in my kurta sarwal, dodging potholes and cows, shouting at tuk-tuk drivers and tourists, and then up the Patan hill on the other side of the valley. I would pick up my work at one of my many international development agencies, and then I would plunge down that hill and cross town once again to go to the next international development agency on my schedule that day.

At night, my girlfriends and I would follow the festivals—an ethnomusicologist, a Sanskrit scholar, an archeologist, a couple of anthropologists—

their arms heavy with recording equipment and cameras and notebooks. I never completely understood their academic explanations, so I immersed myself in the crowd, tried to lose track of who I was supposed to be.

Once I floated up out of the crowd and found myself alone on top of the Boudha stupa with another wanderer for one long moment.

I email an introduction for you: "These are my friends."

I try to remember all my favorite places, my secret spaces, moments I want to share with you from afar. But I have forgotten all their names, if ever they even had names. Of course there are the usual places, the monasteries in Boudha, the Bhairab in Durbar Marg, the Kumari in her palace, the carved windows of Patan Square. I think Swayambhunath is overrun and Pashupatinath is overwhelming. But I like the quiet of Teku. The piles of pigment in the Newari thangka painters' studios. The flower and spice markets early in the morning. The bangle shops. The way the early morning mist hangs in the air.

"Where are the quiet spaces?" you ask me.

I cannot tell if you are teasing me.

The quiet spaces reveal themselves only at 4 a.m., when the grand-mothers come out with their stainless-steel plates of flowers and rice and tika powder to make their morning puja rounds. I know you never sleep. That is the time you should walk.

By the end of the day, you will see through the din of horns and bicycle bells, the crowds casually veering to wind around temples and shrines—men on bicycles on their way home from work, tiffins swaying from handlebars; children in uniforms holding hands on their way home from school; whole families together on motorcycles—hands reaching out to touch the deities' foreheads as they pass.

It is hard to imagine irreverent you so close to the divine. I wonder how this city will affect you.

I am oddly happy and light at the thought of you tracing my foot-steps, connecting with my friends. I was there, at Indigo Gallery's opening reception. I skipped up and down those hallways, and I sat in the balcony windows with my tea. I wrote in the garden that is now Mike's Breakfast. I run my hand along the cool whitewashed stucco of this old Rana Palace, and I accidentally brush against your fingers across time and space.

Rereading Han Suyin's *The Mountain Is Young*, I am nostalgic.

A friend tells me that the word nostalgia derives from a wound that has not yet healed.

I do not know if one ever recovers from Kathmandu.

I am nostalgic for you.

I see your long legs walking, striding across my city, camera held close to your chest, as I jog to keep up by your side. We are both outsiders who somehow can belong here, can blend in here, can just be here.

There is so much I want to show you here.

This is such a romantic city, such a sacred space.

This is a city that changes you.

I couldn't write for years after I left. I thought there was something wrong with all the other cities in which I lived. I forgot that I had come into myself. I let another convince me that I had misremembered and misinterpreted all that had happened to me. I did not even have the courage to open the files to reread my writing from that time.

Until I met you.

Today the clear water sluices over my legs as I dive down to examine the tiny stalagmite cities of coral growing up out of the ocean floor, white chrysanthemums bursting, purple medieval castles, ochre brains. Yellow tang and orange-striped humuhumunukunukuapua'a swim stark against the black lava rock. My hair is full of black sand. My lips are all salt.

Born of fire and passion, this entire island is sacred.

A misguided suitor reads my writing and thinks that I like nature.

I rediscover my strength here. Begin to look like myself again here. Long for the touch of your hand on my skin here.

Now I write.

THE CALIFORNIAN

The Californian says he needs someone who grew up in the sunshine, not in grey days and snowstorms and long winter nights, someone with sunshine and sand in her step, the ocean's salt in her long brown hair.

"DID YOU EAT? MEANS . . .
I LOVE YOU."

I show up at your back door with a bento box of pot stickers. I thought you were inviting me to tea, so I had to bring something. Only to find that you were not really inviting me to tea, the pot stickers forgotten on your kitchen counter, as our tongues tangle on the couch.

I am so nervous I can never eat around you.

A handsome young scholar who has started showing up at my back door asks me, between plates of mango mochi and taro steamed buns and curry beef pastries, "Why are you always trying to feed me?"

"I'm Chinese. I can't help myself. This is what we do. We feed people." As I place another plate of summer rolls before him.

The Peace Corps volunteers in Kathmandu are laughing about the Nepali families who keep asking them, "Did you eat rice yet?" Bhat khaanu baiyo? "No, I had noodles." Wrong answer.

"Is the salt OK?" Noon tik cha? "No, a little too salty." Again, wrong answer.

The young Americans hear the words, but they do not understand. Am I the only one here not laughing? It is the same in Chinese. Ni chi fan le ma? "Have you eaten yet?" (And who can forget the soy sauce scene in *The Joy Luck Club*?)

Regardless of whether you answer *yes* or *no* (your answer should always be yes, btw), the aunties will still sit you down at the table, with a fresh bowl of rice, for more.

As the Blacklava T-shirt says, "Did you eat? means . . . I Love You."

He walks through our house with his big hiking boots on. The children—who normally stop every repair man and every guest who unknowingly walk in with their shoes—sit on their beds, eyes cast down, staring at his big shoes. Inside our house. Inside their rooms. He throws open the front door, strides in the front hallway, goes through the kitchen, up the stairs, in and out of each of the children's bedrooms and mine. Rifles through our drawers. Sits on our beds. Uses our bathroom. I wait silently in the kitchen, but listen to every footstep, every breath. When he finally finishes his tour of what was once our home together and comes back downstairs, I offer him a cup of oolong tea with both hands raised. He sneers no as if I am too stupid to know after seventeen years of marriage that he only drinks coffee. Three-year-old Little Brother offers to share his half-eaten banana, perfectly ripe. He knows bananas are Little Brother's favorite fruit, but he tells Little Brother no, he never eats bananas because they are disgusting. Seven-year-old Little Sister offers him a piece of mochi that she made that afternoon. He grimaces no to microwave mochi, too sticky, too much food coloring, not "authentic" enough. Ten-year-old Second Sister offers him a Spam musubi she made for tomorrow's Chinese School picnic. He glances at the plastic take-out containers and the green onion rubber bands on the table she is using to pack them, and he rolls his eyes, unable to believe how low-class his own children have become in my care, to reuse things instead of throwing them away like "normal people," how degrading that they are learning to live frugally like immigrants, FOBs, even as he lavishes his new white girlfriend with $1,000 designer shoes.

I once drove for hours in the dark, lost in a snowstorm, running from my life, running from myself. When the storm cleared, I found myself at the edge of Niagara Falls, the water churning free of ice, an eerie calm. I remember that my grandparents used to live here. I came once when I was a child. My great aunt and uncle still live here, I think. Somewhere. One phone call is all it takes. Soon, little Chinese women in heavy coats with fur-lined hoods and big boots appear out of the mist, trudging through the snow drifts to fetch me in my tears. Soon I am home again, safe in my great aunt's warm house, a big bowl of oxtail soup before me, the same hot sauce my grandmother uses, the same crunchy daikon pickles my mom makes on the side. Defrosting the snow on my eyelashes, melting the fear in my heart.

My mother thinks that no one could possibly be such a terrible cook; I must be doing it on purpose.

After a week at their father's new twenty-eight-year-old girlfriend's house, the children come home looking gaunt and tired. "Now we know why white kids don't like to eat broccoli!" They laugh hysterically as they describe being fed a whole head of broccoli, steamed into submission, not cut, no salt. They are punished when they try to add soy sauce, when they want to use chopsticks, when they simply push the soggy mess about on their plates. I know I shouldn't, but I smile inwardly as I ladle out five big bowls of beef noodle soup—the noodles fat, the beef nuen, the broccoli perfectly crisp. No rebuttal necessary. My children are home again.

FINDING HOME BETWEEN THE VINCENT CHIN CASE AND COVID-19

First I heard from the high schoolers at Chinese School that all their parents were stocking up on rice and bottled water.

Then I heard about the fights breaking out in the California Costcos. Don't mess with Asian aunties.

Weeks later, the rest of America went crazy for toilet paper.

But I am the child of immigrants. So while y'all were #quarantine-baking sourdough bread, I was sprouting bean sprouts, grinding soy milk, coagulating tofu from scratch, sewing masks. Old School.

"Asian students say coronavirus is spreading discrimination at Michigan State University," *Lansing State Journal*
"Coronavirus graffiti at park leaves Asian-American woman 'scared, frustrated,'" *Royal Oak Tribune*
"Local groups respond to aggression against the Asian community," WZZM Grand Rapids

When I first came for grad school, the only thing I knew about Michigan was that this was where Vincent Chin was killed. And I was afraid.

Twenty-seven years old. Chinese American. A bachelor party. A baseball bat.

"It's because of you little . . . that we are out of work," said the white auto worker.

"These aren't the kind of men you send to jail," said the judge.

A $3,000 fine.

All these years I have lived in Michigan, I have held it at arm's length, felt like I did not belong, waited for the day I could finally return home.

Then I learned about all the people who came together across differences of race and ethnicity demanding justice for Vincent Chin, the people who still speak out to defend others today, the people who would craft a new answer to the question Vincent Chin's mother asked, all those years ago,

"What kind of law is this? What kind of justice?"

"Chinese Americans in Michigan donate more than 200,000 masks, supplies," *Detroit Free Press*
"Michigan leaders encourage reporting of anti-Asian American hate crimes amid COVID-19," WWMT West Michigan
"Opinion: Hate has no home in Michigan, especially in coronavirus crisis," *Bridge Magazine*

As the hashtags surge #StopAAPIHate #washthehate #IamNotAVirus #hateisavirus #StandAgainstHatred,

And Big Gretch starts trending,

I feel, for the first time in all these years, like I belong here. Like I am not alone here. Like this can be home here.

Even as the last snowstorm of the season sweeps in.

But in choosing to call this place home, we have to make this home for all of us, all our communities Asians4BlackLives #FlintWaterCrisis #RunWithMaud #JusticeForGeorgeFloyd #JusticeForBreonnaTaylor.

What will you do to create community, the Beloved Community, where no mother ever has to ask, "What kind of law is this? What kind of justice?"

ADVENTURES WITH THE HAIRCUT AUNTIES

On our way to see the haircut aunties a week before Chinese New Year's, we run into our little friend Miss Hu (who the kids say should go to medical school so that she can become Doctor Hu). We take a picture together and tell her to come with us to see the haircut aunties, just a block away. She laughs and shakes her short hair, "No thanks, I already got my lecture this year."

A week before Chinese New Year's, we all pour into the little shop with the hot pink awning to see the haircut aunties. To me they ask, "Are you going to New York to see your boyfriend? Or to catch a new boyfriend?" They lecture me on how I need to dress up better and spend more time doing my hair in the morning and, please, put on some makeup for once. They blow out my hair so big and glamorous I do not recognize myself.

A week before Chinese New Year's, the haircut aunties tell my daughters to find a nice Chinese boyfriend with a good job. Preferably an engineer. "Look for the nerdy boy who works hard and makes lots of money. Not the shiny boy who knows how to talk all romantic—shiny boy is OK for boyfriend but not for marry. Don't be like your mom."

A week before Chinese New Year's, the haircut aunties tell us about a lady they set up with another customer. "Hey, how come you never set me up with anyone?" "Oh she gets her hair permed, so she's in here all the time. And for a long time. So we sent him in to keep her company while she was under the hair dryer." And now they come in together to get their hair cut. So that's the cost of love: an old Asian lady perm.

Years later, in college, my daughter tells her new roommates that she would like to try bangs, but she knows that the haircut aunties would never allow it. "You know how you tell the haircut aunties how you want your hair cut and then they just do whatever they want?" Her new roommates from New York City say no, wide-eyed.

The World's Most Exciting Date

I tell him right off I do not think I should sleep with him. So he keeps waking me up every time I doze off.

Poignant Truth, Precarious You (and Preparing for the Sriracha Apocalypse)

A moment Before grad school, my father said, "You need one good teapot and a set of good teacups, because sometimes you just need a good cup of tea, in just the right cup." So, San Jose Japantown, store after store, until we found the perfect teapot, right shape, right size, royal blue with a splash of white calligraphy, a bamboo handle, and eight matching blue and white cups that fit perfectly in your hand.

I was set.

Until a white neighbor accidentally broke my teapot and insisted (over my not-just-being-polite protestations) on replacing it. She went to the fancy kitchenware store at the mall and bought me an expensive, garish new teapot. To her eye, it was blue and white, just like mine, but really it was Blue Willow.

Do you know Blue Willow? The world's most popular china pattern ever, designed in 1790 by Thomas Minton in England and sent to China and India to be manufactured (a process that Europeans could not replicate for hundreds of years, by the way) for the black fermented tea dust that Chinese and Indians would not drink. The Blue Willow pattern so perfectly captured the Western imagination that they even invented a romantic legend of star-crossed lovers to go with it.

Afterwards.

The rich daughter of a powerful Mandarin falls in love with a poor scholar, a love so doomed that on the eve of her arranged marriage to a fabulously wealthy duke, the young lovers steal away, pursued by her furious father and his soldiers from the Oriental house with the upturned roof, past the weeping willow tree, over the rickety moon bridge, onto little boats in the bay, and, finally, with nowhere else to turn, they transform into a pair mandarin ducks and fly away.

So tragic. So poignant. So much Orientalism in my kitchen.

(And you know how the dishes you don't like never break.)

A moment

We first meet in Maneesha's sun-drenched kitchen. I watch her warm brown hands as she measures and makes tea for us on the stove. One cup water, one cup milk, one teabag, a handful of spices tossed in as it boils. A perfect two cups of chai. Practiced. Precise. Certain.

After I go home, drunk with curiosity about you, I keep trying to make chai.

But I am not precise. I am not practiced. My chai never turns out right.

So I keep drinking cup after cup of bad chai, the empty teacups stacked to the sky, just so I can read the little fortune cookie messages on each tea bag tab, imagining they are secret messages you are sending to me from wherever you are in the world.

My heart is precariously perched.

A moment

My parents wake me in the middle of the night. Chi lai, chi lai, hurry! Only enough time to grab my favorite doll and I have been bundled bleary-eyed into the car and we are driving. Through the three tunnels that mark the way, then burst into the light and cacophony that is old LA Chinatown at midnight. We always come in the back door, through the kitchen, past the uncles with their giant woks and oil. Tsah! Our eyes adjust to the darkness of the restaurant, then—Aunties! Uncles! Little Friends! Xiao Yeh Time! That means o-ah, xiao long bao, zhu er, hong you chao shou, zhou.

But first we order xiang pian cha, which I always thought was champagne tea. Which makes sense.

These days, teenage girls gather around my kitchen table and I ply them with mango mochi and xiang pian cha, pretending not to eavesdrop as they celebrate college admissions ("I got into MIT!"), gasp over who is sending whom naked Snapchats (Ewww), and cry over "My mom says I'm not allowed to date those steezy third-generation, snapback-wearing, California Asian boys with the expensive shoes."

A moment
    Late 2008
    I walk up to the food bank gripping four-year-old Little Brother's hand a little too tightly.
    I hesitate when I see the food rescue truck unloading there. I hope Jason isn't driving today. (I used to be the development director.)
    I do not belong here.
    The woman at the food bank looks at my wool coat and faded leather gloves and asks, "Are you here to volunteer?"
    I do not belong here.
    With four children, I am entitled to four bags of groceries. I try, but I cannot even manage to fill one. There must be others who need this more.
    Dented cans of off-brand soup, canned vegetables I did not know people actually ate, expensive crusty organic day-old bread from the trendy bakery in town that I could not afford even when I used to have money, giant mutant carrots, meat we do not eat, and cheese we cannot eat. I am allowed one juice box and two chocolate bars. The ladies keep trying to give me tiny little bags of instant rice. And teabags.
    I do not belong here.
    What gets me through is the thought that maybe afterwards, I will be able to write about this and sell it to *Newsweek* for $150, a week of groceries.
    Or maybe I can sell it to *Huffington Post*—for exposure!

A moment
    a year ago election day you were on the train, sending yourself across the miles to me. just for one moment you were real in my arms. today i

loiter at the train station, soaking in the sun and hoping to catch a glimpse of your shadow emerging from a train, any train. as if sheer will could conjure you into form. a new suitor was caught in a freak bank robbery yesterday, and i am unconcerned. instead, i think of you. he writes to me of distance. i write to you of time. i wish you would make time to come see me. i want to touch your cheek and run my fingers along the edges of your ear. i want to feel the weight of you pressed up against me. i want to sit in a café and listen to your stories past midnight, your hand on my knee. explain to me again why you are not here? i do not understand how time keeps moving forward without you.

A moment

Hey! I am finally, officially, an adjunct lecturer at the university! I even have an office! AND a library card! And free tea and reception leftovers in the faculty lounge!

My dad doesn't know how precarious adjuncting is and thinks that I have finally made it. Professor.

The other adjunct in the department laughs, "Welcome to the exploited labor classes!"

A moment

I stare at the *New York Times* society page my girlfriend has emailed to me. "Isn't this your friend?" I knew this day would come. And I knew that I would be sad. But we were just talking last week. You sent me a four-smile smiley face. And you didn't mention that you happened to get married the day before. Just six weeks ago we were discussing San Francisco, and you said you wouldn't be able to make my reading because you would be out of the country again, not because you would be married by then. You even told me that love is a statistical outlier, irrational behavior and self-delusion, and you always keep yourself under tight control because a hot mess is not hot at all. And I am the one who feels embarrassed. Naïve. Ridiculous. Foolish. Not that I want to get married. Not that you owe me anything. Not that there was ever any future there. But. I thought, I thought we were friends. That we had a connection. That we were the sort of lovers who would always circle back to one another. There was kismet to our timing. Our paths diverged and converged right at those moments when we needed each other most. And you always reappeared right when I was on the verge of letting you go.

Or did I imagine all that?

Beyond moments

Philosophically, I don't believe in marriage and promises of forever. Philosophically, I believe in the moment.

I tell my girlfriends that you are the ultimate exercise in staying in the moment. It is what it is. You are who you are. And it is OK because I am my best self when you are in my heart.

It has nothing to do with you and everything to do with you.

But in real life, I feel as precarious as a tottering stack of empty teacups marking all the time and longing that stand there between us.

My friend the desi poet sees me sulking in the café and sits down with me. I pour my heart out to him over a real pot of tea until the water runs white, lukewarm, the rim of the cup stained brown with your memory.

My friend the desi poet explains truth in rebellion to me, "White boys go get hookers. Brown boys eat beef."

Today at the Chinese grocery store, Little Brother, now ten, takes my hand and shows me that truth often lies beyond the moment. "We should buy some Sriracha," he says. "Why?" I ask, since Santa just brought us four cases at Christmas, and he whispers, "You know, for the Sriracha Apocalypse!"

LEARNING TO DRIVE DEFENSIVELY

The night before George Zimmerman is acquitted for the shooting death of seventeen-year-old Trayvon Martin, Little Brother refuses to sleep, waiting up for me to come home late from a research trip to the top of the tallest mountain in the world and back. I am shattered with altitude sickness, and Little Brother wraps his arms around my neck and kisses my face. "You're the best mommy in the world. Really you are."

The night before George Zimmerman is acquitted for the shooting death of seventeen-year-old Trayvon Martin, Little Brother is nine years old, tall for his age, and beautifully brown from swimming under the summer sun. The aunties all coo over him—"xiao shuai ge"—and he blushes with embarrassment as they heap another serving on his plate.

The night after George Zimmerman is acquitted for the shooting death of seventeen-year-old Trayvon Martin, I teach my sweet and naïve multiracial nine-year-old baby boy how to take off his hoodie, slow down his movements, keep his hands visible, steady his voice, and make himself small in front of police and strange white men with guns.

The lessons about strange white women will come later.

Little Brother tells me about his friend, Officer Gold, the African American police officer who comes to his school to read colorful storybooks about spotted police dogs.

And now I have taught him how to hide everything that is good and pure about himself.

Many months after George Zimmerman is acquitted for the shooting death of seventeen-year-old Trayvon Martin, a police car is parked in the snow outside our neighborhood grocery store late one Friday night after Chinese School. As we walk in, Little Brother immediately takes off his hoodie. He says, "Mommy Mommy, take off your hat, take off your hat." It's the middle of winter in Michigan; I don't want to take off my hat. "Mommy Mommy, take off your hat." I am so tired and distracted that I do not notice how frightened he is as we walk up and down the aisles looking for salsa and tortillas for xiao yeh. "Mommy Mommy, take off your hat."

By the time we get to the checkout, he is such a wreck that I finally notice and ask the cashier why the police had been there. She said they were helping an old man who was intoxicated.

Little Brother does not know what the word intoxicated means.

When we get home, I try to reassure him that police are supposed to help us, that he does not always have to be afraid.

But how does a nine-year-old tell the difference?

How do any of us?

When he was five, I remember taking him to the police station downtown so that a police officer could reassure him that the police don't arrest people for no reason, that even if his father wants them to arrest his mother, people have to be suspected of breaking a law to be arrested. He wants to believe his father. He wants to protect his mother. How could we have imagined that his father would call the police on him when he was only thirteen for being asleep in bed and not hearing the doorbell? Luckily, the police said no.

Today, Little Brother is sixteen years old, six feet tall, a mop of #quarantinehair, and learning to drive. As he jokes that he is a Master Driver, I tell him that driving takes a lot of trust. You trust that other drivers will stay on their side of the road, you trust that other drivers will stop at the stop sign, you trust that other drivers will follow right of way. (Thank goodness we believe in science and do not have to worry about gravity.) We talk about what to do if he gets pulled over by the police.

You learn to drive defensively because you do not really know the others. Yet you trust.

Uncle Chien gives Little Brother an old beater car, a sixteen-year-old boy's dream, and after months of quarantine, he is READY. Ready to set forth into the world.

But with COVID-19–inspired anti-Asian American violence, anti-Black and Brownness, police brutality, angry white men with AR15s, and coronavirus, too, I sort of like quarantine. I can teach Little Brother about the Vincent Chin case and #StopAAPIHate and #BlackLivesMatter and #Asians4BlackLives, but I am not ready. Not ready to trust the world.

CRYING ON AIRPLANES

Note: Written on an airplane the week ProPublica released those audio recordings of children crying after being separated from their asylum-seeking parents at the border

Whenever I hear children crying on airplanes, I always laugh. Been there, done that. Ain't got to worry 'bout that no more. (Not that my kids ever cried on airplanes).

I laugh because I don't have to carry two extra changes of clothing in case they throw up on me, twice. I don't have to walk laps up and down the aisle with restless toddlers. I don't have to carry extra sweaters, blankets, clothes, snacks, books, games, toys, videos, headphones, batteries, socks. I don't have to try to sleep with little feet in my ears and elbows in my boob. I don't have to carefully pack and double-check all the children's suitcases and carry-ons so that SOMEONE doesn't try to sneak on her triathlon medal in order to "test" TSA's metal detectors.

I'm done.

But this summer, when I hear little voices crying on airplanes, all I can think about are the cries of those 2,300* little kids ripped from their parents' arms and shipped on cold metal airplanes across the country to literally who knows where, cold air blowing on top of their heads as they fasten their seatbelts and return their tray tables to the upright position.

When all their parents wanted was what every parent wants—asylum, safety, freedom.

And here I am worrying about my eighteen-year-old daughter sitting alone, a few rows behind me.

And I'm done.

---

* more now

WHAT EVER HAPPENED TO 王大中 (WANG DA ZHONG)?

hat ever happened to 王大中 (Wang Da Zhong)?

We meet in San Jose on the first day of Saturday morning Chinese School. On the pages of Book 1, Chapter 1 of the same textbook they use in Taiwan. Instead of "See Dick. See Dick Run. Run Dick Run," we walk to school with 王大中.

"This is my bookbag."

"This is my pen."

"This is my chair."

We all rise and bow to the teacher together as she enters our classroom.

"Good morning teacher."

"Good morning students. Are you 王大中?"

"Yes, I am 王大中."

My parents were born in China, grew up in Taiwan, then came to America for graduate school, like so many of that generation. Pushed by war, pulled by education and opportunity, made a life among silicon chips and prune orchards.

But none of us are Taiwanese, really. We are wai sen ren, from the outer provinces.

Outsiders there. Outsiders here.

I have only been to Taiwan twice: once when I was three and once when I was nineteen. I ate fresh shao bing you tiao hot out of the oil and dipped in fresh dou jiang early in the morning mist. I watched a Taichung University talent show where a cute boy with a guitar sang about the Boxer and the come-ons from the horse on Seventh Avenue. My new friends laughed when I mixed up new vocabulary words an quan mao and bao xian tao, tong wu and tong xing.

I like to say that we are "Chinese by way of Taiwan."

And the nice white ladies at school say, "Oh, I love Thailand!"

With his iconic short shorts, white sneakers, and green book bag, we knew 王大中.

Not a hair out of place, 王大中 was always nice, always polite, always obedient and guai.

王大中 always knew the right thing to do, and he never had any of the problems we did with not fitting in with the American kids at school or being embarrassed by our Taiwanese designer knockoffs or fighting with our parents who just did not understand.

We were bad Chinese School students who wrote our Chinese School homework every Friday night with a Chinese dictionary on one side and mom on the other side. Every Saturday morning, we guessed our way through exams with radicals and homonyms. We invoked his name in every sentence, paragraph, essay, speech, and skit that we wrote as we slogged through our Chinese School childhoods together, chapter after chapter, textbook after Overseas Chinese Affairs Commission textbook.

Whenever we needed an old friend whose name we knew we could write.

Whenever we needed an old friend to walk with us.

王大中.

Once, when talking to my eleven-year-old son who we all call Little Brother about how our family crossed the strait of Taiwan after the war and clarifying the difference between strait (s-t-r-a-i-t) and straight (s-t-r-a-i-g-h-t), he suddenly burst out, "What?! Taiwan is an island?"

"You don't know that Taiwan is an island?"

"Is that why there's that chili pepper on all our Taiwan keychains?"

Aiya. How did I forget to teach him that Taiwan is an island?

But he knows 王大中.

Another generation later, with the same Overseas Chinese Affairs Commission textbooks from Taiwan, 王大中 comes to life yet again in Little Brother's Chinese School storytelling competitions as he jokes about bopomofo, references the night markets and how Chiufen is the model for Miyazaki's *Spirited Away*, and sings about the beautiful Ali Shan mountain. All places he has never walked.

Yet he sings, "Ali Shan de gu niang mei ru shui ya, Ali Shan de shao nian zhuang ru shan."

Today, a refugee boy from a landlocked country calls me island girl as we walk, and I wonder how much the beautiful island of Formosa walks within me across legacies of colonialism, occupation, transnational migration, immigration, resistance, and revolution.

Where are we from? Where are we really from?

Not a hair out of place, 王大中 is always nice, always polite, always obedient and guai. Even without his iconic short shorts, white sneakers, and green book bag, I look in the mirror and recognize his black hair with a hint of curl. Golden brown skin, fair in the sunlight. Square-rim glasses. But this is not the idyllic Taiwan of our parents' childhood stories. Or maybe it never was.

"Are you a student?" the teacher asks.

"Yes, I am a student," he replies.

"Am I a student?" the teacher asks.

"No, you are the teacher," he says.

I wonder what he would say to the children with the sunflowers in their hands walking to the American border seeking asylum. We are #MoreThanBoba.

And so 王大中 walks with me still as I learn to write my life with bigger words and more complicated characters every day.

HE AIN'T YOU

He's everything I say that I want.

He walks by my café every day, hoping to run into me. He emails to let me know that he is walking by my café every day, hoping to run into me. He sits with me at my table while I write, whether a tall table or a low table, and we talk tech, we talk art. He is happy to meet my friends. He talks to my kids, remembers their names, helps them with their math. He buys me fortune cookies, then photographs our fortunes together. He becomes angry when he learns I am being bullied, being stalked. He tells me I am beautiful. He tells me I am smart. He walks with me across town in the rain. He cannot resist me. He seeks me out. He kisses me when you are gone.

But he ain't you.

A Suggestion of Salt

Ravi Shankar and Frances Kai-Hwa Wang

Yes, Lycra can improve your performance,
    But it feels so wrong to be putting on Under Armour
    with my Hawaiian print skirt for tonight's poetry reading,
let alone shoes.
As the leaves change and the first snow falls, I ask myself again, "Why
    am I here?"
My friends tease that I should turn on the heat, but they all have tenure.
    Already I feel the chill of the next few months rolling in.
No, you and I should be someplace restless and warm, eating papayas
    with lime, salt on our lips and sand in our toes.
It is an accident of history that we are here.

A historical accident that we are dropped in an unasked-for
    womb at an unexpected time, languishing on a coast
or in the heartland in one continent or another, instead of nestled
    in a condor's nest.
Leaves turn to fire before they shrivel in the driveway to crunch
    like pages ripped from old books.
The Buddhists say that each instant our karma is ripening with
    respect to another, from seeds planted in another life,
tended in this one, until the fruit, musky and butter-like in its
    consistency, with peppery undertones in its innermost cavity,
falls to the ground, begging to be eaten. I would feed you chunks
    of such fruit if not for the fact of this distance.

Distance is not a fact; distance is a choice. Rama didn't let a little thing
like distance get in the way of going to Sita (although he then
botched it with his insecurity).

Are you brave enough to risk what comes next for that moment of
flame in my cheeks?

We have the technology—email, text, Twitter, Skype, Facebook,
FaceTime, poetry—to create all the connection and distance we
could want. Who needs karma? Google both our names together:
we were connected before we even knew of the other's existence.

Tonight, I turn off the computer, stuff my pockets with marigolds, and
light the lamps from my room out my door down the path toward
the river where the Canada geese take pause. If I float a diya
down the river, I wonder if it will find its way to you by the sea.

Then all you have to do is follow the trail of lights on this dark night
and walk with me until the moon returns.

It is as simple as clay, mustard oil, wick, and spark.

Imagine the lights are flags for the eyes to sing anthems to, a
place to land a plane in the dark.

To tell you the truth, I was more into Hanuman myself, the
monkey king carrying a mountain in one hand, a mace in
the other,

His magnificent tail a rudder in the wind. He probably could
have knocked Rama cold in a fist-fight but chose instead to
serve him. I find that fascinating

When power acts against its own best interests. And what I
wouldn't do for a prehensile tail, one that could serve the
purposes of another appendage, to grab

And coax that flame in your cheek to a blaze. I remain amazed
at the way these simple letters can track miles and years,
carrying

With it a part of you, a sliver of me, the essential core of us, the
not-yet-happened and the imagined song, to a place of
perpetual motion.

I was first told the stories of Hanuman in the Himalayas by people
   with no power, people amused by the powerful's incompetence to
   identify a simple herb. I traded them stories of the mighty Sun
   Wu Kong, master of seventy-two transformations (except for his
   tail), fireproof, immortal, troublemaker, king, kept in line by a
   golden crown.

My grandfather gave me these stories in a cramped Ontario apartment
   when I was ten, yet I, too, once gave up my power for a golden
   crown and behaved in obedience to its pinch.

I follow the news of a young boy of color walking across your campus at
   Halloween, a sword across his back. I have the same sword, have
   walked across campus many times with it, practiced in the alley
   behind Philosophy with it. I did not know how lucky we are to
   be alive, merely arrested for other people's fears, once again given
   away by our inability to transform our tails completely.

What kind of place is this that the son of a professor cannot walk across
   campus without police and SWAT teams being called? What
   kind of exercise is this that I am watching the real-time newsfeed
   and Twitter feed of some distant poet's town? #CCSUlockdown

I look forward to your letters too much.

I wake up every morning at 3:30 a.m., too cold to sleep, too sleepy
   to work, so I reach for my phone in the dark to read your most
   recent poem again.

And then the gulf of time—does even the passage of a few weeks
   diminish the movement else add to the longing, making a
   fetish of it, sprinkling desire with a little juju, dollying it up
   with a dollop of abracadabra

the way a buffalo is a provider, the wolf a pathfinder, the bear a
   shaman and the mountain lion a warrior in certain Native
   mythologies. The emic attribution of value to an object like
   this keyboard with such swift currents

running from the mind to the fingertips to thoughts of you.
   Turns out the alleged shooter was a boy wearing a
   Halloween costume three days after the pagan celebration
   had been zealously candified. He had a samurai sword and
   a mask and a
fake AK because, well, why not? Isn't that freedom of expression,
   or would he have been arrested if he wasn't Black? And the
   Twitter flames fanned. And the dockets bred fear. Gave
   proof to the right that the frisk is still here.
Students alternately terrified and used to it, gun culture being
   part of their upbringing, this the third or fourth lockdown
   they had sat through in their young lives. What would
   Hanuman do? Instead, I'd like to leave this suggestion
of salt as a reminder for you.

There you are. I thought that you had disappeared.
Funny that you reappear today, on Thanksgiving Eve, just as I sauce my
   vegetarian ba bao sticky rice stuffing, my mother's voice in my
   head, "Soy sauce is not salt!" Yet she would not approve this secret
   pinch of salt that you bring me, pink with 'alaea clay and the
   caress of the sea.
Nor are any of my girlfriends impressed, as they hover in my kitchen
   debating the faults of all my suitors as if I weren't here, dismissing
   you most disappointedly of all, "Mr. Monkey Tail."
I have traveled through thousands of stories since last we were here in
   the space of this poem, now uncertain how to continue.
There is no debate or uncertainty among the civil rights activists sitting
   around my kitchen table. Here, where a nineteen-year-old girl
   of color, Renisha McBride, knocks on a door seeking help after
   a car accident in the night and gets shot in the face. Here, where
   community-wide vigils and protests are needed to arrest the
   white man who killed her. Here, where I review with my children
   again how to talk to strangers and police—don't run, keep your
   hands visible, take off your hoodie, walk with a friend, be careful

of the night—knowing full well that another Halloween past, sixteen-year-old Yoshihiro Hattori was wearing a white tuxedo while standing on the sidewalk with a white friend in the afternoon when he was shot and killed, the white man acquitted, his fear of the Other understandable.

My children nonchalantly explain to my friends the secret codes and annoying protocols of school lockdowns while in another room their teenage girlfriends squeal over a latest crush, and there you are at the door, with a song and a kiss of salt in your hands.

Monkey tail indeed! You know in some versions of the *Ramayana*, like in Bandung & West Java, Indonesia, Hanuman is the hero. Not Rama. This simian dazzling in anklets is not slavishly devoted to his master but has an army of acolytes of his own to worship him although the reason he is so revered is because he was brave and humble. Did you know that the name Hanuman comes from the Sanskrit hang- which means "chin" and mat- which means "excellent." So literally he was the "one with the awesome chin," like some Superman screen star with whorl of lock on his forehead. Really it is because he survived a blow from Indra. But I'll demur and grin to see if the shape of my imagined jawbone might just conjure your hand.

Still many don't know that he had another name also—Maruti, or "born of the wind." OK so now I'm going to get real desi- geek on you and drop it like it's doxa or at least a hot dosa off the griddle, a dosage of the dopest saga till Sega went gaga with Sonic at least according to some priestly sorts, the ones who wear white linen even in the video arcade. The ones who bathe in the river. I'm talking about mad skillz this Ravana- stomper had: anima, to shrink (in the pond we'd wound up on); maxima, to expand (swelling with slippery touch); lagima, to become weightless (waist a sail, ankles spurs); garma, to grow planetary in size (keening plums, thrumming

tongues); brapti, teleportation and celestial acquisitiveness
(inside the outer layer, unpeeling with forefinger and thumb);
parakmya, irresistible willpower (mutual feasting); vastiva,
just the mastery over all creatures (invisible tremulous
leaping for the sun); and istiva, to grow godlike with power
to destroy (rampart shaking). Forget Daredevil with his
echolocation and Cyclops with his concussion beams, the
magnificent monkey tail is where it's at!

Oooh, The Poet transforms. I like that.

I once saw Superman and Sun Wu Kong side-eye each other in a
three-year-old preschool class, measuring who was the most
powerful. Puffy fake muscles and assimilationist disguise versus
jing gu bang and tiger-skin skirt. Little Brother holds out his
staff and shouts, "Bian!" his face confusion when his command to
transform does not work.

My girlfriend Sujata's son does not ask to celebrate Christmas like the
other desi kids. No fool, he asks if they can celebrate Chanukah:
eight days of presents trumps one.

I am too amused by my own cleverness.

Bound and hanging limp above yet another bubbling cauldron, the
monk Tripitaka is kidnapped in every chapter, every episode,
every story, by yet another demon wanting to feast on his
flesh. And he simply waits with eyes closed, lo mi to fo, to be
rescued again by Sun Wu Kong, fearless, faithful, and fireproof.
Sometimes I feel as alone as Sita when Rama gives her up, with
no recourse but to call out to the earth for redemption. I call
out to lawyers, teachers, principals, social workers, psychologists,
secretaries, police—but I am caught in too many battles on too
many fronts. I wish I could be all heart and kindness and belief
like Little Brother, free to do more than defend myself, my arms
up around my head.

I long for a champion like Hanuman or Sun Wu Kong to stand by my side
and fight alongside me. I had hoped that champion might be you.

The thing about those ancient myths, which I read in knickers
and undershirts in my grandfather's house under the
sweltering sky, the lemon burst of the sun making us all
wince, was that there was such a clear delineation between
good and evil, might and frailty, but in the world there are
gradations, a range of hues that make even the vilest villain
a human nonetheless, that make the most sanctimonious
monk a sinner. Isn't that the grand realization, that we all
fall short of our ideals and therefore we are closer than
we ever imagine, irrespective of skin or song or tongue
or family?

Sometimes I read articles on physics to make cocktail
conversation. Recently I read about a new "quasi-
particle" dubbed the leviton and that proved the quantum
mechanical effect of anti-bunching because it dispersed like
waves rising from the surface of the ocean. I confess I'm
like a magpie looking for metaphors to pluck and put in my
own nest, to keep me stimulated in the winter. But let me
ask you, what is the difference between something that is
fundamental and something that is emergent?

I digress. I regress. I confess that I transgress in my mind because
the stone in the ground stays in the ground, but the one
that skips on the waves sinks. Flies before it sinks. And that
moment of levitation is worth the bottom of the sea for all
eternity.

Plus your cleverness amuses me as well.

No, Poet, I do not agree. Our ancient gods and heroes, spirits and
sprites were not Charlton Heston's God, flaming bush and
booming voice. They were jealous, greedy, bloodthirsty,
competitive, lazy, mischievous, flawed as we. Yet they draw us
taller. The Catholic nuns dismissed all my stories with one word:

"pagan." I had to cross the oceans to rediscover the power of the gods, the reality of our stories, to learn to walk tall again with our heroes at my side.

Is there any difference between fundamental and emergent, other than when something was discovered, and by whom? Like Captain Cook discovering Hawaii, Vasco da Gama discovering India, American foodies discovering Korean fried chicken, mainstream publishing discovering writers of color? We have always been here. We know our histories and our stories, even if others do not. #notyourasiansidekick.

My teenagers only just figured out what Manjusri and his consort have been doing in that thangka painting in the hall.

Your poem arrives as my friends and I are trimming our "Christmas branch" with selfies and Sriracha. They have decided to set me up with an uptight academic who thinks internet dating is safer (wha??) and with "Sweaty yoga shorts guy" (ewwww). These are not stories for the ages. I want a story with one who would search through 10,000 lifetimes for me, a story with one who would risk eternity on the bottom of the sea for me.

For I know what it is to be a stone in the ground. With only honor to sustain me, I stayed away from stories then, stories that gave me hope and breath. Then one day he threw me away, and I found myself flying through the air, skipping over waves, drowning in the surf, transforming like Sun Wu Kong and Hanuman in the glint of sun and sea from stone to fish to flying fish to dove to hawk to phoenix in flames. At last my head can be in line with my heart.

So tell me another story, Poet, full of your shiny things.

Falling, Mad and Alone

You are mad, out of control, reckless.

What is so wrong with you that you fall in love so easily? How can you be so unhappy as to mistake me for any sort of solution? I am not anything special. I am just younger; I am just here.

We met for a few days in a snowstorm. Now you say that you love me, you say that you miss me, but how can that be when you barely even know me? I push you away with both hands and tell you that isn't possible.

But you run after me and insist that you know. You paint me as pouring my heart into your life. You fill up my phone with dozens of bright-red heart emojis. And you tell me again.

Maybe there is something wrong with me that I cannot bear to hear it. Maybe it is because no one has said those words to me since I was twenty-five years old (and even then, it was in French, so I'm not completely sure, LOL). Besides, what do we know about love at twenty-five? What do we know about anything at twenty-five?

You seem so alone. Not lonely, just alone.

I feel it in the way you fill the world up with words, how you surround yourself with people, the frenetic pace at which your art keeps surging out. There is a physicality to you that is both bulwark and camouflage. You wear it in your shoulders, a heavy Carhartt against the barbs that strike and shape men of color. You tell me you need an audience. Perhaps I just need the attention.

I remember how I never felt so alone as when I was married, with four little children and a dog, three jobs, on every committee and task force, always busy, always driving, always surrounded by friends.

So many secrets in those days.

When my husband left me for a woman twenty years younger, I suddenly discovered how many people in our small town were sleeping in separate bedrooms, emailing each other from upstairs to downstairs, sneaking out of the house to breathe. They couldn't help themselves, they had to tell someone, they all told me.

"Put my address into your phone and your glove box," I counsel every woman. "If you need to, come to my house, any time day or night."

And with the men, I come to recognize a certain squirm and mumbled deflection in response to my too-obvious questions—"Weren't you living with someone up in Vermont?" "What does your wife think about that?" "Why would you apply for that job on the other side of the country without talking with her first?"

It has been years since I've thought about the cormorants with the colorful rings around their necks. These graceful long-necked birds are trained to leap off small fishing boats and dive deep into the water to catch fish in their beaks. The colorful rings around their necks keep them from swallowing their catch. The fisherman reaches down the bird's throat, brutally pulls out the wriggling half-swallowed fish, then sends the bird obediently back into the water for more.

And the cormorant with the colorful ring around its neck is grateful to have had the taste of fish on its tongue.

Once upon a time, that was my life.

You want to rescue me. You keep trying to rescue me.

But I tell you over and over again that there is no rescuing me. There are some things that cannot be avoided, some burdens that simply must be borne. My path is rough, but it is mine to walk.

Still, you give me solutions, give me advice. "I can't help it, I'm a man," you say gruffly as you reach for yet another way to try to save me.

I see you.

I actually think you are the one who needs rescuing, although you cannot see it.

I want to shout—Save yourself! Save your art!—but don't delude yourself into thinking that there is any future with me. I am inconstant and will not be there in the end for you. I am only a warning sign that something in your life is amiss. I worry about all that you don't yet know about me.

Be careful with your heart, my friend.

Then in the lonely hurt of morning, I wonder if I am really as strong as I project. (The first time my husband had an affair, two months after our wedding, he said, "I didn't think it would bother you, you always talk so tough.")

That is not the kind of life I lead now.

I keep no secrets. I tell no lies. I don't sneak. I don't make promises.

I remember what it is to be so starved for affection that one conversation with a stranger in a snowstorm had once been enough for me to fall and fall hard. But now I am exhausted trying to not imagine a cozy domesticity that will never be, trying to not be persuaded by your certainty, trying to create distance even as we sculpt this space between us with tongue and teeth and Chinese ink.

Every night at midnight, you write me long winding messages, full of funny stories, madness, and song. By late afternoon, I manage to talk myself out of you, to pull back, to reassert my certainty that you are madness. But then evening comes and your name pops up on my phone again. And I smile, curious and caught.

I do not want to be the one calling out to you, but when you show up at my front door, I cannot turn you away. Despite everything that I say, I look forward to your messages too much. Against my better judgment, I find I am growing fond of you.

I am falling.

And you are not there.

You Cannot Resist Me When
My Hair Is in Braids

Sitting in Sweetwaters Café for the afternoon with a pot of Earl Grey tea, trying to write, trying to put off looking for a day job, trying to figure out how to construct a new beginning out of all this financial ruin, all the while watching the cute boys walk past my window on this cold grey day, wishing for some handsome young professor to walk in and flirt with me for a bit.

I've got my hair in braids today. You cannot resist me when my hair is in braids.

Tiny Modern Love Songs

He walked with me in the long loneliness that was my marriage, invisibly, silently, handsomely. He sat in the empty passenger seat and held my hand as I drove the kids to school, swimming, soccer. He listened to all my rambling stories, was simply present. Only he wasn't. Merely a memory from long ago, a ghost of a love not followed, I clung onto the lilt of his voice in my head, the way his gaze once fell on me. I dared not seek him out in real life. Instead, I sought the courage to remember who I once was.

"What if I asked if I could kiss you?" All I can think is, "Why would you want to?" It has been so many years since I sat this close to a beautiful man, and I suddenly realize that as the mother of four children, busy with school and driving and PTO that—other than teachers, principals, and my ex-husband—I have not even talked to a man in ten years. And here is this beautiful brave brilliant man wanting to kiss me in front of the whole world. I am not ready. I am heartbroken before we even begin.

Hey, I'm getting married soon! I can't wait to meet him. You see, my mom went to see a monk. In Texas. Who told her I am getting married. The monk even gave her a date, which she won't tell me. But soon. Now, because my mom only knows of one single man, she wants to introduce me. "You remember, they stayed at our house when you were four and you complained that the baby cried all night. He's a doctor now." A crying doctor! Great. Now she thinks that I must have a secret boyfriend she doesn't know about.

DTW

I love traveling alone,
   Early morning, quiet airport, high heels in my hand.
   My thoughts wander curious: where in the world might you be . . .

"It's Not a Yellow Dildo!"

They find me hanging in a doorway at the end of the hall. I am wearing a long white flowing gown, my feet bare, my long black hair wild across my back. Carved into my chest is the name of the psychologist that drove me to it. So. Tragic. So. Dramatic.

I let myself linger over this brutal fantasy. It is perversely satisfying, like picking at the edges of an itchy scab.

I know I am indulging myself, but don't worry. There is no danger of me ever hurting myself because I went to Catholic schools. And if there is one thing they teach you in Catholic schools, it is that you cannot commit suicide. I saw the movie. Besides, when I think through the steps of actually picking up a knife and carving the seven letters upside down and backwards into my skin, "Ouch!"

And black Sharpie simply would not have the same dramatic effect.

Looking every bit the prim, old fashioned schoolmarm, with her long wool A-line skirts and bulky embroidered sweaters, the psychologist was supposed to help us.

Instead, she sits in her high-backed leather chair and tells my oldest child—the one who took second-year Japanese at the university during her freshman year of high school—that studying Japanese is bad because it leads to an interest in manga (which she pronounces man-ga), which leads to pornography and sadomasochistic behavior.

My fifteen-year-old daughter, no fool, responds, "Have you been to the romance section of Borders lately?"

The psychologist tells me that my eighth grader is a leader. Yes, she certainly is. This child is the leader of the children. OK, fair enough. This child is like a gang leader. Wait. What? Hold on there, lady.

Quote: "And gangs are an Asian tradition, too, you know."

To me, she says, "I know you've been raised to be submissive to men," and then tells me that my children would be better off if I did not exist. W.T.F.

Don't worry, though, she knows what she is talking about because her son played tennis in elementary school, so some of his best friends were Oriental.

Remember that scene in Maxine Hong Kingston's *The Woman Warrior* when the narrator asks where that stereotype of the Quiet Chinese Girl even comes from? Because Chinese women are not quiet, Chinese women are loud! She describes Chinese women in Chinese restaurants, all speaking Cantonese at once, with its guttural tones and hard edges, each one louder than the next, spit and food flying out of their mouths, dishes clanking, the whole restaurant shaking.

As soon as I read this, I realize that I come from a family of women, with at least thirty aunts and great aunts, each one stronger and louder and feistier than the next. And even with so many real-life examples right there in front of me, the stereotype was so ingrained that it never occurred to me to even ask the question.

Or perhaps something changes when Quiet Chinese Girls grow up to become Fierce Tiger Moms?

For years I used to stem the spinach for him, carefully pulling each leaf off each stem, then hand ripping the leaves and throwing away the stems, despite how appalled my mother was at such waste. Because he did not eat spinach stems, because he knew better than me, because the American way was better than the Chinese way, because he was the husband.

Then one day, I stopped.

I first encounter a banana-case Tupperware in the lunchbox of a three-year-old Japanese American boy in Little Brother's preschool. Curved yellow plastic to keep the banana from bruising, round airholes to prevent overripening, and cheerful lettering in Japanese and English spelling out "banana case." This. Is. Brilliant! Best. Thing. Ever. Invented.

Just what I need to keep Little Brother's favorite fruit from turning into a puddle of brown mush in his lunchbox.

But not available in the U.S.

I try to mimic the design by poking holes into various sized Tupperware and bento boxes, padding the square corners and round hollows with napkins, not closing the lid all the way. But nothing works.

I beg every Japanese family I know to please bring me a banana case back from Japan. No luck.

Years pass.

Then, at the Banana2 Asian American bloggers conference, Bicoastal Bitchin' hosts a party at the Far Bar to launch their new website celebrating Asian American sexuality, YellowDildo.com. They give away plastic banana cases as swag with their URL, YellowDildo.com, wrapped around the middle. I forget my conference cool instantly, with my big hair and foul mouth, and revert back to my true identity as somebody's mom, "OH! A banana Tupperware! I've been looking for one of these for years!"

Little Brother does not understand why his teenage sisters scream when they find the swag in my suitcase, or why they all suddenly beg to have bananas for lunch, but luckily we manage to convince him (since he can't read yet) that the URL says yellowduck.com.

A few days later, Little Brother figures out that it can't really say yellowduck.com the way his sisters are going on about the "bad word" on it. He whispers to me that he has finally figured out that really it must say yellowdumb.com.

He knows that this very bad word is not allowed in our house, so he mouths it soundlessly.

Yes. Very bad word. Yes, Sweetheart, don't say that word.

At twenty-two, I was such an old maid that my parents were so relieved that SOMEONE ANYONE was willing to marry me that they did not ask too many questions. He was tall and he was going to be a professor. That was enough. That he promised to learn Chinese was a bonus. (He didn't tell us that he was hopeless at learning languages.) I wore a bright-red embroidered qi pao for the wedding in front of two hundred of my family and family friends and six of his, no veil.

My family tried to set me up with a Nice Chinese Boy in a last-ditch effort before the wedding, just to be sure. His family tried to set him up with a Nice White Girl because he was their last chance for white grandchildren. We thought we understood cultural differences and stood above them.

He used to laugh at me for saving and reusing take-out containers, refilling water bottles, and reusing Ziploc bags. He said he recycled enough in the '70s, before recycling was cool, so he didn't have to anymore; and he made it his mission to eat all the chocolates that other Chinese people gave us to finally take them out of circulation. He joked that we should trade partners—I should marry the Chinese American boy who worked for him, and he should marry the Chinese American boy's white girlfriend who also complained about too much Tupperware in their kitchen.

When he left me seventeen years later, he told me that he was leaving because I am Chinese and all my friends are Chinese.

My immediate reaction was to create an Excel spreadsheet of all my friends, broken down by ethnic, racial, and religious backgrounds.

Two years later, he married that girl.

"Now what is this I hear about a yellow dildo on your kitchen table?" asks a child psychologist friend.

"It's not a yellow dildo! It's a Tupperware!"

The children had accidentally found (and intentionally deleted) the photos on his phone, so we already knew he had come inside our house and taken pictures of all our rooms. But we had not realized that he had sent the pictures to the psychologist who then told others in our small town's psychology community that I keep a yellow dildo on the kitchen table.

One day, the banana case disappears from Little Brother's lunchbox, and the girls and I search for months—our house, our car, the school lost and found, their dad's house, their dad's girlfriend's house—and we can only find one half of the banana case—the side with the URL on it—that I had kept safely at home. (Well, obviously, I wouldn't send that half to school in a seven-year-old's lunchbox!)

The next school year, their father finally admits that he threw it away, "because it was disgusting."

When my friends at YellowDildo.com hear the sad sad tale of how our beloved banana case was lost, they send me a dozen more. I am careful to not give the children bananas on Daddy Days, but one day I forget. And it does not come back. Curious. The next time I forget, it also does not come back. And, strangely, the third time I forget, too.

The teenage girlfriends giggle at the daily lunchtime installments of the Great Banana Case Wars. "Your mom is such a troll!"

People always ask me if he was having an affair. Of course he was having an affair! But I didn't really care. The shock had long worn off after the second or third one. Now, you have to understand. I had four little children under ten. I had been either pregnant or nursing nonstop since 1994. I was tired of being agreeable and accommodating and pawed at all day and all night. I was tired. I wanted to sleep. Those of you with little children understand. I figured if she was f***ing him, then that was one less thing on my to-do list, ten less minutes of pretending (yawn) "ooh ooh baby baby," ten more minutes of precious sleep.

The day I turn forty, he squints at me from across the room and says, "You look old."

He sits down heavily at the optometrist's office and furrows his brow. He is concentrating hard as his twenty-years-younger-than-him-girlfriend, our former babysitter, gives him her report over the phone. She must be going through Little Brother's lunchbox again, reporting on all the terrible things I packed for his lunch. Then he stands up and walks across the optometrist's office to me and says, "You have to stop putting those yellow dildos in his lunchbox."

"It's not a yellow dildo, it's a Tupperware."

"You know what it is," he says.

"Yeah," I say, "It's a Tupperware."

"You know what it says on it," he says.

"Yeah," I say, "It says 'banana case' right on it, in English and in Japanese."

"If you keep putting them in his lunch," he says, "I'm going to keep confiscating them and keep throwing them away. I have photographs."

"Yeah," I say. "You have photographs of Tupperware."

The veins in his forehead start to bulge as he shouts, "I will make it a problem for you. I have photographs. I will send the photographs to the court, and I will make it a problem for you!"

I am suddenly aware of how quiet the optometrist's office has become. The children have evaporated, stifling giggles in the corner behind the glasses display. The optometrist is adjusting an elderly couple's glasses, staring down hard at the frame in his hands.

And we are shouting at each other in the optometrist's office. About Tupperware.

This is what has become of my life? This is not a life, this is absurd.

For the first time in all our years together, I stop being defensive, I stop trying to help him. I stop responding as the obedient Chinese daughter, the good Asian wife, the accommodating problem-solver extraordinaire. Maybe that is why our story has become so surreal. I have gone off script, somebody else's script, and it is time to save myself.

"You need help," I say. And then I walk away.

Talkin' to Whypipo

His memory appears unexpectedly on the page during a Sunday afternoon timed writing exercise.

The night he showed up at my door during college wearing full Navy whites. Simply because I had made some clichéd crack about having a weakness for a man in uniform. How did he even come to have a full Navy uniform, anyway, just hanging around in his closet?

It would not be my thing today. But I was nineteen, he had blond-brown wavy hair, and he was trouble.

One date. Laughing and splashing around campus in the dark.

After that I have no memory.

Before the timer even rings, I have messaged my girlfriend across the country to see if she knows what ever happened to him.

And of course she knows.

And she says he is single.

Shoot, I forgot to warn him that I write about everyone that I meet.

How do I tell him that I don't date white guys? Nothing personal, it's strictly political, an identity thing, been there done that. And what would people say? I have a reputation.

The last time I made one exception, I was chatting away at Sweetwaters Café downtown, when my girlfriend Taz published her article, "Why I Don't Date White Guys." And there is her headshot, filling up my whole phone, her royal blue blouse bright, her big brown eyes staring straight through me.

I turn my phone over guiltily, but my phone keeps blowing up as hundreds of friends around the country keep commenting and that date quickly grinds to a halt.

He is so white.

(Say it with me: how white is he?)

He is so white that he goes to Renaissance faires. Like, a lot of them.

He is so white that he teaches Shakespeare.

He is so white that he rows crew.

He is so white that he has a massive hipster beard way beyond its sell-by date.

He is so white that he lives in Los Angeles and from his Facebook pictures appears to have only white friends. How does anyone even do that?

He is so white that he lives in Los Angeles, Asian American foodie heaven, and he eats salad. Kale salad. When I tell him that I don't eat white people food, he doesn't even know what I mean.

He is so white that we get into an argument about affirmative action and model minority myth right off the bat.

He is so white that as he tries to dip a toe into my world and name-drop prominent Asian Americans, all he hits are the ones I have gotten into big public fights with.

And I know, I know, #NotAllWhitePeople. And I know, I know, some of my best friends are white.

But still.

He is so white.

And somehow, in spite of myself, he makes me smile.

This is why I don't date white guys. This is why I don't even talk to whypipo if I can help it. Nothing personal, it's strictly political, an identity thing, been there done that.

I'll talk to neighbors and old friends. I'll talk to white folks who are a somehow "other" and get it.

I have learned to make small talk about the weather.

But sometimes I wonder if it might be easier to navigate white spaces with someone like him at my side.

Meanwhile I have a crush on a too-handsome, too-young poet of color in my town, IRL, much more my usual style, about whom my friend Rohin says, "OMGGGG, Frances, HOW OLD IS HE?"

At the end of the Facing Race conference, the biggest race and social justice activism conference in the nation, thousands of us activists of color spill out of the second floor Cobo Hall ballroom. Everyone was there, a big tumble of colors and textures and styles—whether we are talking skin or hair or fabric or clothes or head covering or cute shoulder bag. A group of young African Americans begin drumming and dancing on one side of the doors and a Native American storyteller holds a circle of people spellbound as he sings a story on the other side.

Across the open space of the great staircase, a formal Marine ball is just getting underway in the opposite ballroom. Thousands of young white men with close-cropped hair, crisp blue dress uniforms, and shiny black shoes—children, really—march in, sharp and polished. On each one's arm is his "girl," skinny and pale, teetering on stiletto heels, wearing a long formal strapless prom dress, all primary colors, corsage on wrist, blond curls piled atop her head.

They are coming into our space—where we have laughed and cried and shouted for the past few days—on that side of the hall. As we are leaving from this side of the hall. Our paths do not cross.

The contrast is stark. I feel it in the pit of my stomach.

I overhear one older Asian American activist ask a young white Marine, "Where are you from?"

This is America. This is my world.

I tell my old whypipo friend this story, a story connecting his past to my present.

And he cannot see.

3 A.M. WITH ERHU

Full moon shining in through my window wakes me at 3 a.m. I get up to check on the lava, and the sky is RED. Faint Chinese erhu melodies float in through my window as the neighbor practices across the way. And I reach for my phone to see if you are there.

Down in the Basement
of the DIA

Down in the basement of the DIA, we discover the museum's
stash of old film reels. Shelf after shelf of old film canisters
unfurl before us. Tucked into dusty grey boxes bound tight with
thick olive-green straps, raised white letters popping out of red Dymo
labels.

I run my finger along the pressed white letters, feeling for the hesita-
tion of days long past.

Classics. Art films. Sci-fi. Horror. Noir.

You spot an old favorite and take it down off the shelf, ask if I have seen
it. I was too afraid to watch it, I confess. We will have to watch it together,
you say, tucking it under your arm. I am surprised by your confidence, to
mention any future beyond this moment.

Yellowed old movie posters stare down on us from the walls—*Casablanca*,
Blue Velvet, *Godzilla*—from before when they were new.

As we look through the rest of the film titles, our heads tilted to the
right, I imagine forward to later tonight after the museum has closed,
after tonight's films have been put away, after the audience has gone
home. How you will show one last film past midnight, just for me, like
the local boys who worked at my hometown movie theatre used to do
for the girls that they liked.

I was never one of those girls.

Suddenly, the fluorescent tubes above our heads wobble and go out.
Without thinking, I reach for your hand. Feeling the cling of the damp
basement cold, I am relieved when your hand clasps back.

I realize that I haven't held hands with a boy in the dark of a movie theatre since I was twenty-two years old. Was it *Hamlet*? Such a simple joy, holding hands in a movie theatre. I have gotten used to seeing films on my own now, when the kids are gone, every Thanksgiving and Christmas day.

Together we find our way through the darkness, around bookcases and down passageways and up and down staircases, until we find our way into the light once again. The Chinese traditional orchestra is performing on stage, the lion dancers preparing to go on next. You and I stay hidden in the wings.

Later, as we step out of the backstage door, my hand still firmly clasped in yours, I am surprised to find the sun still out, people walking on the green grass, the whole world still ahead of us to discover.

THE SPACE BETWEEN GOODBYE

L ingering on the front porch steps at midnight, after a night of art and climbing snowdrifts, two friends hug goodnight and prepare to part ways. The ice-encrusted branches glisten like glass in the streetlamp's gaze. One more story before I go in. Then one last hug, and in the space between goodbye, a kiss I thought was headed for my cheek lands unexpectedly on my lips.

Hidden in the safety of the night, I hesitate, then let myself be persuaded, let myself kiss back, until we are hungry like teenagers, his face in my hands, my teeth on his lips, until a car rounds the corner and catches us in its headlights, our friendship transformed in that moment as we step apart and look away, feigning embarrassed innocence.

I feel him shivering beneath his coat and see that he has no gloves. It's twenty-three degrees out and snow is beginning to fall and catch in my hair. This is ridiculous. I should let him go or let him in, but I am not yet ready to think that far. I always draw the line at my front door. But I don't want to lose this moment.

So I linger awhile longer in this space, this space between goodbye.

Earlier in the evening, I watch him do what he does and there is nothing better than watching a man of color own his art and command his space and fully realize who he is. Brilliant. Beautiful. Butterfly dancing in blue light.

Usually you see it coming. Usually you have a sense of it. Usually you either hope or dread how the night might end. You wonder whether you and he are on the same page, wonder whether he will try, wonder whether you want him to try. And you negotiate. With crisp handshakes, faces turned at the last moment, standing a little too close or a little too far, breath hanging in the air, a casual tug on his coat collar, silent vows about next time or never again.

But sometimes you get it wrong. Sometimes he surprises you completely. Sometimes you surprise him.

And then the moment is over, and I am enveloped back into the light and warmth and safety of my house. Shoes off in the foyer, a quiet cup of jasmine tea alone at my kitchen counter.

I usually don't even let men know where I live, let alone let them walk me home and linger on the front porch step.

The next morning, the moment over, I go back to work and life, distracted. We have said goodbye and he has gone and I assume that that is it. I have no expectations. It was only a kiss.

But then he calls and he writes and he sends me a song—he sends me a song!—and I find myself growing fond of him.

I try not to read too much into any of it, I try not to think too far ahead, I try to protect him from what he doesn't yet know about me. I try to linger.

And in the quiet before goodbye, I sing his song.

SECRET CRUSH

I wish I would have had the nerve to have taken you for a walk along the water last night. I would have liked to have walked with you and shown you the river, especially with the moon so full, heavy like a ripe hachiya persimmon, silver skin translucent, ready to burst, but I had already started disengaging from the moment, creating distance, creating space, and I was afraid.

For someone who talks so much about staying present in the moment, I sure know how to create distance.

Sitting next to you in that lecture hall was electric, every accidental brush of your elbow against mine, the way you leaned into me to ask my thoughts, the pressure of your shoulder against mine. Am I imagining this? Are you leaning into me or am I leaning into you? I finally had to extricate myself to go hide in the bathroom to text a friend,

"I AM MELTING!"

My friend's response, "Hydrate, hydrate, hydrate!"

You don't know, but I've had a crush on you forever, since the first time we met, so many years ago.

At the time, I was still in shock, just coming out of heartbreak and marriage. It was a wonder that I managed to pull on boots and even get to that lecture that S insisted I attend.

At the time, my imagined criteria for dating was that a man be willing, willing to go out with me.

My father laughed when I saw the possibility of dating or even marrying again someday. No. My father was surprised enough that someone was willing to marry me the first time, since I had been so old at twenty-two. But now, with four children and an angry ex, he said that all any man will

see when he looks at me is four college tuitions. No man would be willing
to take on that much debt. Stop dreaming. Be realistic. No man will ever
want you. You have to survive on your own.

Then I met you, and you were everything that I didn't even know that
I wanted. Tall, handsome, smart, brave, creative, kind, community activist,
Chinese American, bilingual, bicultural, not too old, and not too young.

And married.

But that did not matter as I was mostly so amazed that someone like
you could even exist, so much like me and who I wanted to be, so much
of what I didn't even know was possible. I told everyone that I had met
the perfect man, that the perfect man exists, and that that was enough.

If there exists one, there must exist another.

First Date Protocol

I always make sure to tell my dates that I write about everyone that
I meet.

Discretion is not my strong suit, but if I like him, I will try to protect
him, to disguise and to hide him.

One date is so freaked out that he stops talking for fifteen minutes.
Dead silence. Not one word. While I keep driving straight ahead.

Another date is intrigued. "Oh, what do you write about?" Then gives
me a string of pornographic suggestions to write about him.

What they do not realize is that for me, what is public is not real.

What is real is not public.

I am searching for someone who can read through my illusions and
find what is hidden in my stories.

My children laugh about my public persona. "I'm Frances Kai-Hwa
Wang, I do what I want."

How I wish I really were my public persona.

Instead, I shift between the public "Frances Kai-Hwa Wang," the
everyday "Frances Wang," the legal "Frances K. Wang," the Chinese
"Wang Kai-Hwa," and the personal "凱華." I am tired of explaining the

differences. I am tired of being the bridge between cultures. I want to find someone who can read me, just as I am one of few who can read the hundred different things encoded in your Chinese name.

My father once told me he does not care what is written on his tombstone because the transliterated name he has used for the past fifty years is not his real name.

I cannot explain the disappointment I feel when Chinese people call me "Frances"—which feels ridiculous because it is my name, too—because really I want to retreat into the quiet of "凱華" for a little while.

A friend goes with me to Chinese School, where she is promptly cornered by a bunch of Taiwanese moms who demand to know, "Why did Wang Kai-Hwa have to marry a white guy? She is so pretty. She is so nice."

Have to? What? Pretty? How?

Maybe because no Chinese parents would let their precious protected ABC sons near me?

When you marry a white guy, white people think you are trying to marry "up," but the Chinese aunties know it is because you are a failure as a Chinese person. Too tall, too awkward, talks too much . . .

The first time I heard someone talk about her experiences growing up in a Japanese American concentration camp, I cried all the way home. I had read about the incarceration of Japanese Americans during World War II in books, but to hear it firsthand . . .

She told many stories that day, but the one that hits me hardest takes place after the camps. In her first job as a young adult, her coworkers are so suspicious that they follow her every time she leaves her desk, even to the drinking fountain, even to the ladies' room, even to the boss's office where she asks, "Is this company policy that everybody follows me?"

I thought about all the old white people in my life—teachers, neighbors, mentors—and I feel betrayed to realize that they are all of the same generation. Outwardly, everyone is very nice and polite. But how much of the old suspicion remains? How much of our socialization remains hidden? How many people have I trusted and loved with this kind of unconscious undertow?

I once did a poetry reading at a bookstore that had also invited the Ladies' Auxiliary Club to come read. The room was half my people and half little old white ladies.

As I read "The Beauty of Brown" about a beautiful Brown boy and the color of his brown skin against mine, the little old white ladies start to giggle nervously and shift in their seats. The mood quickly becomes sultry and hot.

For me, this is a story of identity. For them, it is a story of the forbidden.

The bookstore owner jokes about the dirty dreams all these little old white ladies are going to have tonight about Brown and Black men.

I'm not sure how I feel about that.

Our paths cross every few years, and I squeal and minor fangirl every time. I tell my students and my children about him, teach his books, tell his stories.

The perfect man exists, and knowing that is enough.

If there exists one, there must exist another.

What is public is not real, what is real is not public.

My mother puts out a call to all my older cousins to set me up with one of their friends before my birthday comes and it is "too late." My mother tells my cousins that money doesn't matter, education doesn't matter, race doesn't matter, breathing is enough.

Then in some mangled air traffic delay, our paths cross again in a crazy long layover at an airport, both of us in the wrong city, both of us just passing through, both of us in a bubble. With nothing else to do, we talk, just talk, talk for hours, talk for days, and he is even more perfect than I knew; and I am happy, just happy, happy for weeks. My neighbor sees it in my face right away, remarks on how the glow lingers.

As we talk through one of my poems, I realize that it is not just that he is tall and handsome and smart (although that is a big part of it). It is an identity thing—more than conversation, more than intellectual compatibility, more than language, more than physical attraction (although there is a lot of that too), but in getting to know him, I get to know myself. In understanding him, I understand myself. In wanting him, I want myself.

I am so curious.

This is so awkward.

Why does he have to be so virtuous?

Images of what a life with him might look like flash through my imagination, accented with quiet bowls of jook early in the morning light, beef noodle soup at midnight, seamless family reunions where people can actually talk to him, mutual friends, shared interests, events made tolerable by the other, no need to explain or to translate. I wonder "how Chinese" he really is and how much I am projecting.

I realize I have already crafted that life with my children, where we can function fully in English and in Chinese, with whom I do not have to segregate parts of my life, who make me better than I am, who can codeswitch and keep up, always.

But they are children.

It's all I can do to not tweet, not shout, "SOMEBODY STOP ME FROM PROCLAIMING MY SECRET CRUSH ON THIS PER-FECT MAN."

After two and a half years of not being able to write anything creative, I finally start writing again.

I AM SO DISTRACTED! All I want to do is write poems.

I was unhappily married for a very long time. I have a lot of experience with loneliness and unrequited affection, gaslighting and cultural kan bu qi. I fear I do not need much to be content. I am tempted to poke, to ask how happily or unhappily married he might be. I have my suspicions. I could guide him. That is what a good friend would do. But I dare not. I can't be that one.

So I am writing.

And that is enough.

It has to be enough,

she says publicly in a poem.

SOWING AUNTIES

He laughed at me and my family for saving and reusing—tofu containers, green onion rubber bands, plastic bags, twist ties, take-out containers, glass jars, cookie tins—and he took it upon himself to secretly throw away all that we had carefully saved and washed and stored away. He thought it made us small and poor to reuse. He was big and rich enough to go out to the store to buy things new.

He even opened and ate all the boxes of chocolates people gave us as gifts, "to take them out of circulation," before we could regift them to someone else. (Regifting wasn't even a word then, it was just normal).

He said he did not have to recycle because he recycled enough in the '70s.

When I speak to Asian American student groups and tell them that there are people in the world who throw away all the green onion rubber bands and then go out to Office Max to purchase new rubber bands, the entire audience gasps.

At any auntie's home, the world comes full circle. Shoes off at the door. Stacks of tofu containers by the kitchen sink, green onion rubber bands

looped on the faucet, plastic bags full of plastic bags, kitchen towels sewn
from rice bags. Twist ties in the chopstick drawer, giant soy sauce can
under the sink. Big detergent containers and cardboard boxes carefully cut
into new shapes for new purposes. Old children's toys transformed into
tools couched in memory. "Have you eaten yet?" 你吃飯了嗎? as code.

Auntie greets me wearing a blue monkey Aeropostale sweatshirt I
remember my cousin wearing in the '90s. We eat from plastic Hello Kitty
bowls and plates, the same ones we used when I was small. The secret
cupboard full of candy and red envelopes is still stocked, I checked. When
she sees a tear in the knee of my jeans, she tells me to fetch her cookie
tin so she can mend it. She lets me go "shopping" in her closet. She sends
me home with a huge pile of leftovers packaged in a variety of plastic
take-out containers and vegetables from her garden wrapped in last week's
Chinese newspaper.

Auntie does not think in environmental terms. She does not calculate
the economics of her garden, full of the flavors of home that she cannot
buy, from jiu tsai to persimmon trees. She fertilizes with eggshells and tea
leaves, and her garage is full of dried seeds for next year. Despite a long

successful career in America, she still does not buy anything full price. When I buy her a CSA for the quarantine so that she does not have to go to the grocery store so often, she complains that $16/week for vegetables is too expensive.

Auntie fights with the heron who hovers by her pond. "Those are MY fish, not the bird's fish."

We never talk politics, but my mom told me that my dad (who had always voted Republican) came to her in a dream and told her to vote for Bernie in the primaries.

My daughter goes to college with a big box of old mismatched bowls. Her housemates are mortified when a blue and white noodle bowl breaks because they think they have broken an antique family heirloom. True, that bowl was once her grandmother's, then mine, then her uncle's, then hers, but it is more hand-me-down than heirloom. (Heirlooms are for white people.)

At school, my daughter studies the science of climate change and environmental sustainability.

My daughter likes to search for treasures in vintage stores and thrift shops.

My daughter buys from sustainably and ethically sourced companies.

My daughter teases me for the Marie Kondo–resistant clutter in my house, where a stack of tofu containers sparks joy. Yet I find that same stack of tofu containers by her kitchen sink, holding the soap, holding some coins, holding a few ripe tomatoes from her garden.

My daughter borrows Auntie's sewing machine and sews masks for all of us by trimming the ends off of old Hello Kitty tablecloths, cutting apart old baby clothes, "shopping" for fabric in Auntie's sewing room. My other daughter finds old flowerpots and seeds at Auntie's home and begins growing her own #quarantinegarden from bok choy ends and green onion roots. Little Brother bikes and bikes and bikes.

I come from a long line of aunties, each one stronger, smarter, and feistier than the next. Six sisters in my grandmother's family, six in my mother's family, three in my father's family, at least nine cousin aunties, a few married-in aunties, countless friend-of-the-family aunties, and still more

aunties back in China and Taiwan that I don't know. My children have all these plus my generation scattered across the continents.

Aunties may look cute and sweet on the outside, but never underestimate what is on the inside.

Only aunties are able to coax tropical plants out of the snow-covered ground.

Only aunties are able to take on rude white men twice their size and make them cry.

Only aunties are able to keep us all rooted and fed and supplied in #quarantinetoiletpaper, creating home half a world away from where they were born. While keeping up with everything and supporting everyone back home, too. Global interconnectedness is not new for us—we overhear it in our mom's phone calls every week, and we help carry big boxes of it to the post office every holiday.

As our aunties and uncles and parents and grandparents get older, we watch as they walk slower and begin to forget their English. We take them to the grocery store and go with them to doctor appointments. We beg them not to sneak out during COVID times. We worry about the long-term effects of the bombs that fell all around them during the war. We wonder how the trauma of war and famine and poverty and racism have been passed down through the generations.

These are things they never talk about, except as jokes.

"And we thought the bomb fell on your Auntie, but then we found out it fell on the cow!" Ha!

"Because of the war, there was no milk, only rice gruel. That's why I'm so short!" Ha!

"I had a picture of my daughter on my desk at work, and this white man said, 'Reminds me of a girl I knew in 'Nam.'" Ha!

We are the children and grandchildren of immigrants and refugees. We carry more with us than family recipes, a second language, and hand-me-down homemade clothes. We can never be as frugal, as hardworking, as smart, or as able to find a deal as our immigrant and refugee elders, but we have seen them fight for us. We have seen them sowing stories to grow a life for us here.

During hard times, we know it can be done.

And we know who to ask for help.

BREATH RISES

These pandemic days, I rise early at six every morning to walk the dog, check my tomatoes, and practice tai chi sword. I love walking around the block alone, the whole world empty and new, fresh and crisp with dew. No mosquitos. With four children, this is my one chance every day to be alone. Quiet. For a few moments, no one else exists in the world, even as I check out all their vegetable gardens.

After eight, the grandmas and grandpas start coming out, slowly, one at a time, then the runners and dogwalkers and stroller people and bicyclists and cars emerge. The highway sounds marking the end of the neighborhood accelerate. And I am pushed back into the world of sound and motion again.

My father always planted an enormous vegetable garden, but I never paid any attention until this year's worries about food supply chain disruptions and #quarantinegarden trends. And like my Ba, an electrical engineer who always overdesigned everything, I was all Go Big or Go Home. Three cubic yards of compost. One hundred seventy-five square feet of garden. Mostly greens (gailan, bok choy, Chinese chives, arugula, mizuna, shiso, red-in-snow mustard) and tomatoes. Lots of tomatoes. So many tomatoes. The deer, woodchucks, raccoons, squirrels, chipmunks, and bunnies have eaten everything else. I don't mind. I am happy to share. (I am especially enjoying secretly leaving little baskets of tomatoes and basil on people's porches. This is the one plane where I do not worry about not having enough.)

Earlier in the spring, while everyone was #quarantinebaking, I was sprouting bean sprouts, grinding soymilk from scratch, coagulating my own tofu—just like the aunties taught me—and thinking of all the ways our elders adapted and saved and reused and survived when they first came to this country. Sometimes we gently tease our immigrant and refugee elders, "Do you really need these three thousand plastic take-out containers and green onion rubber bands?" But with national shortages of toilet paper, flour, masks, gloves, elastic, canning lids, and even coins, who is laughing now?

And I am happy.

Breath rises.

A friend once told me that you should never speak your deepest darkest fears out loud because by uttering them into the world, you write them into existence.

That is the power of putting words on your breath.

For seventeen years, I never dared to utter my deepest darkest fears out loud.

Then one day, I asked myself, "Why am I so afraid?" And tired of the weight of secrets, I whispered my deepest darkest fears into the ear of a mathematician as we walked down the alley behind Common Grill restaurant in Chelsea. He laughed at me, thought my fears preposterous, my unhappiness ridiculous.

Then, I held my breath, but nothing bad happened.

Then, two months later, just as I was about to dismiss my friend's warning as silly superstition, my whole life came crashing down upon me.

But breath rises.

These past few years of President 45 have been nonstop PTSD for me. Been there done that. Unscrupulous businessman who does not pay his vendors. Bad businessman who chooses bankruptcy as business strategy. Rich businessman who has plenty of money for lawyers but none for his obligations. No accountability for broken promises and broken contracts. Wild, death-defying lies. Terrible spelling. Stalking. Unexpected racism and conspiracy theories. "The problem with you is that you are Chinese and all your friends are Chinese." Constant. Gaslighting. Facts do not matter because I cannot afford to pay the lawyers and psychologists and social workers to actually read the evidence. Facts do not matter because every convoluted thing he says is believed. Facts do not matter because as an Asian American woman, I am suspect for not being demure and grateful. The one time his friends see me and the kids out on a Saturday night at the art museum reopening with a handsome dark-haired friend, he takes me to court the following Monday to bully me back into submission. He complains to the court that I take the children to the art museum, the library, and to see documentary films. Meanwhile, I almost lose my house three times because of carelessness (or willfulness) on his part. We spend So. Much. Money. on lawyers, mediators, psychologists, and social workers. For him it's worth it. He pays the henchmen and doesn't get his hands dirty as they torture me by threatening the children. I am in So. Much. Pain. I break out in straight lines and lines of shingles. When the henchmen are no longer useful, he stops paying them while I continue to pay off my half of the debt. I learn the hard way that a contract/judgment/court order/invoice (the Constitution in 45's case) is only as good as one's ability to enforce. The state of Michigan has to take away his driver's license and put him in jail overnight before he finally takes child support seriously. The young assistant attorney general asks me, perplexed, "How did he catch up $22,000 of child support so easily?" "I told you, because he had the money all along." No. Consequences. Forget about verbal promises. My children and I take on crushing student and parent loans for four college tuitions that I will never be able to repay. We lean heavily on the generosity of our community for scholarships and social services, even when they look askance at us because they know who he is, they know he has the money. I learn So. Much. About. Power. Meanwhile, he and his skinny young bride are traveling abroad, buying designer shoes, cheating the IRS, and getting ugly tattoos. Remember the chaos of the first presidential debate? That was my life.

If you see him, remind him that he still owes me and his children over half a million dollars.

But that is not the story I want to tell.

Instead, I write about the 5,400 children ripped from their parents' arms at the border, COVID-19–inspired anti-Asian American hate crimes, Asian American activists and artists coming together for Black

Lives Matter, how the wisdom of aunties will save the planet from climate change.

Have you eaten yet? 你吃飯了嗎?

Breath rises.

Big Garry says that I have a much more interesting story to write.

Breath rises.

In Chinese, the term for anger is made up of two characters, 生 sheng (to give birth, to be born, unripe, and uncooked) and 氣 chi (air, breath, vital force). Anger is what happens when all your breath or vital force churns around your insides and rises up transformed.

You do not choose to be angry. Anger rises up inside you.

But if you reverse the order of the two characters, 氣生, anger melts into air.

That is the power of putting words on the page.

Heartbroken, I once filled a notebook with, "I am beautiful, talented, and smart. I am the prize. I am beautiful, talented, and smart. I am the prize. I am beautiful, talented, and smart. I am the prize. I am the prize. I am the prize . . ."

I write myself into existence every day.

And I breathe.

Breath rises.

Epilogue

Lost Constellation

Sometimes I feel lost.

Lost among the stars, you could trace the constellation of my body, the constellation of my life, shattered and scattered.

Arms and legs and hopes and dreams splayed out across the heavens. Lying flat on my back in the grass as my children run and blow bubbles in the sunshine. Lying flat on my back in the street as cars surge past, the breath knocked out of me. Lying flat on my back in a boat, seasick, floating across the planet to a new life free of famine and war.

Coming from one tradition, growing up in another, and choosing to take the best of both to create something new, we stand strong because we are woven out of the stories, traditions, food, and audacity of our immigrant and refugee elders. Not just a cute boy's pick-up line, we are a zigzag path of lights as we forge new identities and create real lives in this place.

The recent surge of violence targeting Asian American elders and women across the country has artists and activists responding with art and creative community-based solutions, interracial solidarity, and allyship. Asian American aunties sew masks for Native American communities, Black and Latino volunteers walk with Asian American elders, and a diverse coalition of activists and restaurants fill refrigerators and donate free meals.

Together with our elders and sisters, we step forward to weave the night sky night after night. Together with our elders and sisters, we step forward and fall in love with this life of work, family, joy, and sacrifice. Together with our elders and sisters and brothers, we step forward to build the bridge of magpies to bring together the Beloved Community where everyone is welcome, seen, fed, housed, reunited.

We are home.

About the Author

FRANCES KAI-HWA WANG is an award-winning poet, essayist, journalist, activist, and scholar focused on issues of Asian America, race, justice, and the arts. Her writing has appeared in online publications at PBS NewsHour, NBCAsianAmerica, PRIGlobalNation, Center for Asian American Media, and Detroit Journalism Cooperative and in *Cha: An Asian Literary Journal, Kartika Review, Drunken Boat, Joao Roque Literary Journal.* She co-created a multimedia artwork for Smithsonian Asian Pacific American Center, and she is a Knight Arts Challenge Detroit artist.